Frank Horvat

Introduction by Virginie Chardin

T&H Photofile

Frank Horvat: Itinerary of an outsider

'A photograph does not only say what its author would like, but also what he says without meaning to.'

Frank Horvat, *Chronique de mes appareils photos*[1]

Frank Horvat has often been described as an unclassifiable photographer. The diversity of his work and experimentation have helped to cover his tracks; indeed it was he who compared himself to a labyrinth or a house with fifteen keys.[2] Throughout his long life, this photographer thought constantly about the meaning of his own work and explained a great deal about it in the writings he left behind. It is therefore not easy to sum up his work in seventy-five images, so we have chosen to let the images speak for themselves. They tell us about the inner workings of a photographer of the body, whose career was marked by several foundational experiences that occurred within the context of the history of photography from the post-war period to the present day. The milestones discussed below mark turning points in the remarkable journey of a photographer of great intensity.

Pakistan, 1952

Francesco Horvat was twenty-four years old and had gained early experience as a photojournalist for the Italian newspaper *Epoca*, the Swiss magazine *Die Woche* and the French magazine *Point de Vue-Images du Monde*. He dreamed of joining the Magnum agency and had visited Henri Cartier-Bresson the previous year. 'Those who consider themselves his students are legion and those who challenge his precepts are even more numerous. I have belonged to both sides, but without him I would not have become what I am,'[3] he acknowledged. The journey of initiation that he began in Pakistan, and which was to continue in India over the next two years, allowed him for the first time to give free rein to his imagination, by seeking out stories to pitch to the press. Following the example of *Life* magazine, most publications and agencies expected photographers to submit complete photo essays, in the form of a series of captioned images, telling a story that could be published across multiple pages. 'The format of the picture story was imposed on all those who wanted to work for magazines, and the most they could do was to take advantage of it, similar to the way the great Hollywood filmmakers took advantage of the constraints of the box office, or the dramatic playwrights of the *Grand Siècle* worked within the laws of the classical unities of drama.'[4] In Lahore, instinct or personal interest led him to the red light district, known as Heera Mandi (Urdu for 'Diamond Market'), which was also the site of an annual festival in which young girls, unveiled and adorned for the occasion, danced for an audience of men, who could bid for the right to talk to a girl's family with a view to a meeting or a marriage: a secular custom that the government of the day was attempting to outlaw. He also photographed smokers of opium and hashish (ill. 5), a particularly spectacular Muslim religious ceremony, and a wedding at which the face of the bride was revealed to the groom in a mirror (ill. 1). He then sent his prints to *Die Woche* magazine and to agencies in Paris, Munich, London and New York.

The young reporter's gamble paid off. His stories from Pakistan and India, under the name Franco Horvat, were published in *Die Woche*, including the front cover of the issue published on 27 April 1953. They were subsequently reprinted in other publications over the course of the next few years.[5] In Spring 1954, he left for Israel and Jordan to photograph the Easter celebrations of the Samaritans (ill. 6), which earned him a place in the pages of *Life*. He then went to spend a few months in London, with a contract from the New York agency Black Star. One of his images of a Muslim wedding in Lahore was selected by Edward Steichen for the celebrated exhibition *The Family* of Man at MoMA, New York, in 1955. Having entered the circles of the international press, the photographer, who now used the name Frank Horvat, was able to return to Paris fortified by experience, which he hoped would suffice to open the doors of Magnum to him.

Paris, 1956

His encounter with Paris was, however, to lead him in a different direction. The place that was, in his imagination, primarily the city of Baudelaire and of Cartier-Bresson, not only offered subject matter for photo essays but also 'entries in the diary of my wonders, my wishes, my fears and my misunderstandings'.[6] It was here that he married Maria Teresa Lorenzetti, with whom he would have three children, and here that he definitively settled.[7] Initially, it was to *Réalités* that he turned. This French monthly magazine, which employed the photographers Jean-Philippe Charbonnier, Jean-Louis Swiners and Edouard Boubat, who would remain Horvat's great friend, also published images by many freelance photographers as well as members of Magnum and Rapho. The editors suggested the subject of pimps and prostitution in Paris, and he became passionately involved. At a distance or hidden behind the wheel of his car, he explored the streets and cafes of Pigalle and the rue Saint-Denis, by night and by day, as well as the paths of the Bois de Boulogne, in a kind of long tracking shot that in many ways recalled the world of cinema or detective novels. On its cover, the magazine proclaimed: 'A remarkable document. *Réalités* denounces one of the greatest scandals of our times.'[8] Frank Horvat's archives contain prints from that time, which were made by Georges Fèvre, one of the principal printers in the Pictorial Service laboratory founded by Pierre Gassmann. At the time, Gassmann was the exclusive printmaker to Magnum and gathered around him many French and international photographers.[9] This photo essay is staggering. Anne de Mondenard and Michel Guerrin, authors of a book on the magazine, considered it to be 'one of *Réalités*' most powerful stories', speaking of 'Horvat's tragic realism'.[10] The theme of voyeurism fascinated him so much that he continued to shoot images of 'Paris by night' for several weeks: the Folies Bergère, a Lido premiere attended by Charlie

Chaplin, Brigitte Bardot and Jean Cocteau, performers in fairground booths, and several striptease clubs. In a masterful series on a club in Pigalle called Le Sphinx, the photographer succeeded in securing the willing and touching involvement of the strippers behind the scenes while leaving the voyeur-spectators to their loneliness. These projects led him to acquire a telephoto lens, which he tried out on the urban landscape. Fascinated by the effects he obtained with it, he left the cabarets behind in order to experiment with views from above, looking down over monuments and intersections where crowds and vehicles intermingled. He was interested in the graphic interplay of signs and signage, street furniture, roofs and omnipresent typography. He positioned himself in the midst of the crowd where he captured close-ups of faces, or crouched down to child height. Frank Horvat showed a selection of these images to Roméo Martinez, chief editor of *Camera* magazine, who was immediately enthusiastic and decided to publish them in a large portfolio and to exhibit them at the First Photography Biennale in Venice in 1957.[11] This recognition was to be of crucial importance in the continuation of Horvat's career.

Jardin des Modes, 1957

Frank Horvat often recounted that William Klein, whose book about New York he had greatly admired, had seen Horvat's images of Paris in *Camera* and had called him to ask about his lenses. It was Klein who then introduced him to Jacques Moutin, art director of *Jardin des Modes*. Moutin suggested that he transpose the style he used for his Paris shots to the field of fashion photography. Horvat accepted, provided that he could work with a Leica and in natural light, as he had done for his reportage work. Following an early series shot in the greenhouses at Auteuil, in 1957 he photographed Tan Arnold at the Chien Qui Fume, a cafe in Les Halles (ill. 27). Then, following the precise instructions of Jacques Moutin who drew up the project for him, he took what was to become his best-known photograph: a women wearing a white Givenchy hat posing in front of a group of men training their binoculars on an imaginary horserace (ill. 29). The freshness of his images caused a sensation

and other magazines requested images in the same style. The shots
of Nico in the Bois du Boulogne, Anna Karina at Les Halles (ill. 26)
and Monique Dutto surrounded by passers-by (ill. 30), published by
Jours de France in 1959, were in a similar vein, as were those of playful
rural or family scenes published by *Elle*. Horvat himself appeared on
the cover of the German magazine *Magnum*, shown photographing
a model with his Leica.[12] After the departure of Jacques Moutin at
the end of 1959, Horvat's contract with *Jardin des Modes* came to an
end. He became an associate member of the Magnum agency, and
a few months later began a regular collaboration with *Vogue* UK.
This situation did not please his associates, and would force him
to choose, reluctantly, between fashion and reportage.[13] In March
1960, for their first collaboration, *Vogue* published a beautiful photo
series in which Horvat abandoned outdoor settings in favour of
the studio. The models posed against a plain backdrop, alongside
musical instruments, stuffed animals, statues and other props. They
included Judy Dent, who was to become one of his favourite models.
He captured her in touching portraits, including a nude that revealed
an intimacy between them. She also appeared on the cover of *Vogue*
in October 1960, modelling a selection of country clothes, in a series
that used Yorkshire locations and local extras: a group of children
outside a row of terraced houses, horses and dogs, churches and wide
landscapes. These images made a great impression on the group of
Swinging London photographers, represented by David Bailey, Brian
Duffy and Terence Donovan.[14] All eyes were on Horvat and, when he
reached New York, he was soon hired by Miki Denhof at *Glamour* and
Marvin Israël at *Harper's Bazaar*. The latter was the most prestigious
magazine in its field and, in 1962, it published some of Horvat's most
iconic images, alongside those of Richard Avedon, Hiro, Jeanloup
Sieff and Saul Leiter. In Italy, Horvat got his models to pose with
groups of men – a recurring motif in his work – or with writers,
artists, politicians and intellectuals, in settings that suggested women
of taste and not simply models chosen to show off the clothes. He
would revisit this concept in the autumn issue, this time in Paris
and with established female celebrities such as Helena Rubinstein,

Marie-Louise Bousquet and Agnès Varda (ill. 38). Horvat often described these shoots for *Harper's Bazaar* as representing the apex of his career in fashion, although he continued to work actively in this field well into the 1980s, publishing interesting work in *Vogue* France, *Stern*, *Vanity Fair* and *Queen*.

Around the world, 1962–63

Nevertheless, Frank Horvat was not satisfied with this type of photography, which was undoubtedly lucrative but did not allow him to express himself as he wished. Fashion itself didn't interest him, and he found the demands of art directors, editors and agencies, with their many constraints, annoying. Models sometimes complained about his insistence that they look natural. Moreover, he found it hard to reconcile the opposition between fashion and reportage that had motivated his departure from Magnum. Deep down, he had not given up on the idea of confronting the reality of the world. Indeed, at the same time, he continued to collaborate with *Réalités*, publishing stories on Algiers, Berlin, London, the Borinage region of Belgium and the Paris suburbs. His complicated private life also made him want to take off again, as he had done ten years previously when he left for Pakistan. An opportunity was provided by a commission from the magazine *Revue*, based in Munich. Its director suggested that he take a round-the-world trip for a photo story on great non-European cities. He accepted on the condition that he would have carte blanche and be able to show the entirety of his work on his return. He was joined by a German writer, Dieter Lattman, who would look after the text. So he sold his Paris apartment, bought a Nikon Reflex and an array of lenses, and set off for Cairo in November 1962. His itinerary took him to Tel Aviv and Calcutta in December, to Sydney, Bangkok and Hong Kong in January, and Tokyo in February. These were followed by Los Angeles, New York, Caracas and, finally, Rio de Janeiro and Dakar in June 1963. On his return, he had large-format prints made by Jules Steinmetz, one of the best printers in Paris, with whom he worked for thirty years.[15] His selection of shots demonstrates a clear interest in self-expression that extends beyond

the documentary interest of the subjects in hand. But *Revue*, which
had acquired a new editor-in-chief in the meantime, only took a
small sample of the selected images. It published these photographs
across ten issues in 1963, with titles of varying punchiness. This
was a disappointment for Horvat, who realized that, in an age when
television was invading homes and fulfilling the general public's need
for images, 'the concept of the picture story was already outdated'.
He also admitted 'less to have borne witness to the world than to
my own curiosities, obsessions and personal preconceptions'.[16]
The series was subsequently reprinted by the Italian magazine
Playmen, while Horvat's images of Rio were published in *Terre
d'images*, whose editor-in-chief was Jean Adhémar, also head curator
of the Department of Prints at the Bibliothèque Nationale de
France. Subsequently, however, these prints would remain in storage
and Horvat would virtually stop shooting photo stories, with the
exception of a few colour images for *Réalités*. It was not until forty
years later that he would reconsider the images and texts of that
time in a self-published book.[17]

Cotignac, 1970

At the turn of the 1970s, the status of photography began to change.
Institutions, museums and galleries became interested in it.
Portfolios were published, practices were put in place that favoured
the establishment of a market in prints, collections were assembled,
retrospectives held. Photography acquired a cultural value. In 1970,
Jean-Claude Lemagny, curator of the Department of Prints and
Photography at the Bibliothèque Nationale de France, contacted
Frank Horvat and asked to see his work. He selected one hundred
and ten images, which he acquired for the library's collections and
which formed a very early retrospective of his work. In the same
year, the Rencontres Internationales de la Photographie in Arles
was established to promote auteur photography in all fields of
photography. That autumn, Horvat saw an isolated house at Cotignac
in the Haut-Var region, surrounded by olive and almond trees, and he
bought it. Although he was still a fashion photographer, he regularly

withdrew there with his partner Véronique Aubry. He started giving
thought to personal projects that would no longer be reportage, and
which would be free from the rules and constraints of commissions.
Interested in colour and inspired by nature, he began shooting a series
of portraits of trees (ills. 65–68). This resulted in an exhibition of
Fresson pigment prints at the Musée des Arts Décoratifs in Nantes in
1977, which also toured abroad with some success. He was encouraged
by this initial project to undertake new experiments, to which he
dedicated himself with a passion. These included *Very Similar*, a
series of portraits of women that made reference to the history
of art (1983), *Entre Vues*, a book of interviews with photographers
(1990), *Bestiary* (1994) and *Mythology* (1996), two sets of striking digital
collages, plus *Photographic Journal*, *La Véronique* and *Eye at the Fingertips*,
all autobiographical collections. All of these images revealed an
insatiable desire to reinvent himself, and it was to an essay on New
York, created between 1982 and 1986, that Horvat devoted his very last
book, just before his death.[18] A meditative reflection on the city and
its inhabitants, about which he noted in his diary on 14 January 1986:
*With my black and white photos, I was after moments that 'told a story'. Now, NY,
I am after 'moments of colour'. […] All I know is that harmonious juxtapositions
are not enough. Maybe the harmony has to be so unstable as to suggest that the
moment is unique.*[19]

Virginie Chardin

Notes

1   Frank Horvat, *Chronique de mes appareils photos*, undated manuscript, Studio Frank Horvat archives, Boulogne-Billancourt.

2   Frank Horvat, *Le labyrinthe Horvat*, Paris: Éditions du Chêne/Hachette, 2006; Frank Horvat, *House of Fifteen Keys*, Boulogne-Billancourt: Intragne, 2013.

3   Frank Horvat, *Chronique de mes appareils photos*, op. cit.

4   Frank Horvat, *Autobiographie*, undated manuscript, Studio Frank Horvat archives, Boulogne-Billancourt.

5   These included, among others, *Sie und Er*, *Paris-Match*, *Picture Post*, *Münchner Illustrierte*, *Le Ore*, *L'Illustrazione Italiana*, *Frankfurter Illustrierte*, *Collier's*, *Esquire*, and more.

6   Frank Horvat, *Autobiographie*, op. cit.

7   Michel born in 1956, Lorenzo in 1957 and Marco in 1961.

8   *Réalités*, no. 127, August 1956.

9   Hervé Le Goff, *Pierre Gassmann, la photographie à l'épreuve*, Paris: Éditions France Delory/Picto, 2000.

10   Anne de Mondenard and Michel Guerrin, *Réalités. Un mensuel français illustré, 1946–1978*, Arles: Actes Sud; Paris: Maison Européenne de la Photographie, 2008.

11   *Camera*, international monthly magazine of photography and film (in German, English, French), no. 1, January 1957; 1st International Biennial Exhibition of Photography, Edizioni Biennale Fotografica, Venice, 1957.

12   *Magnum*, no. 22, February 1959.

13   He became a Magnum associate in 1960 but left the agency in 1961. See Clara Bouveresse, *Histoire de l'agence Magnum: l'art d'être photographe*, Paris: Flammarion, 2017.

14   Martin Harrison, *Appearances: Fashion Photography since 1945*, London: Jonathan Cape, 1991.

15   Frank Horvat, Paris-Audiovisuel, 1989.

16   Frank Horvat, *Autobiographie*, op. cit.

17   Frank Horvat, *Time Machine: Un tour du monde, 1962–1963*, Boulogne-Billancourt: self-published, 2004.

18   Frank Horvat, *Side Walk*, Paris: Atelier EXB, 2020.

19   Frank Horvat, *Autobiographie*, op. cit.

1. Muslim wedding, the groom seeing the face of
his bride for the first time in a mirror, Lahore, 1952.

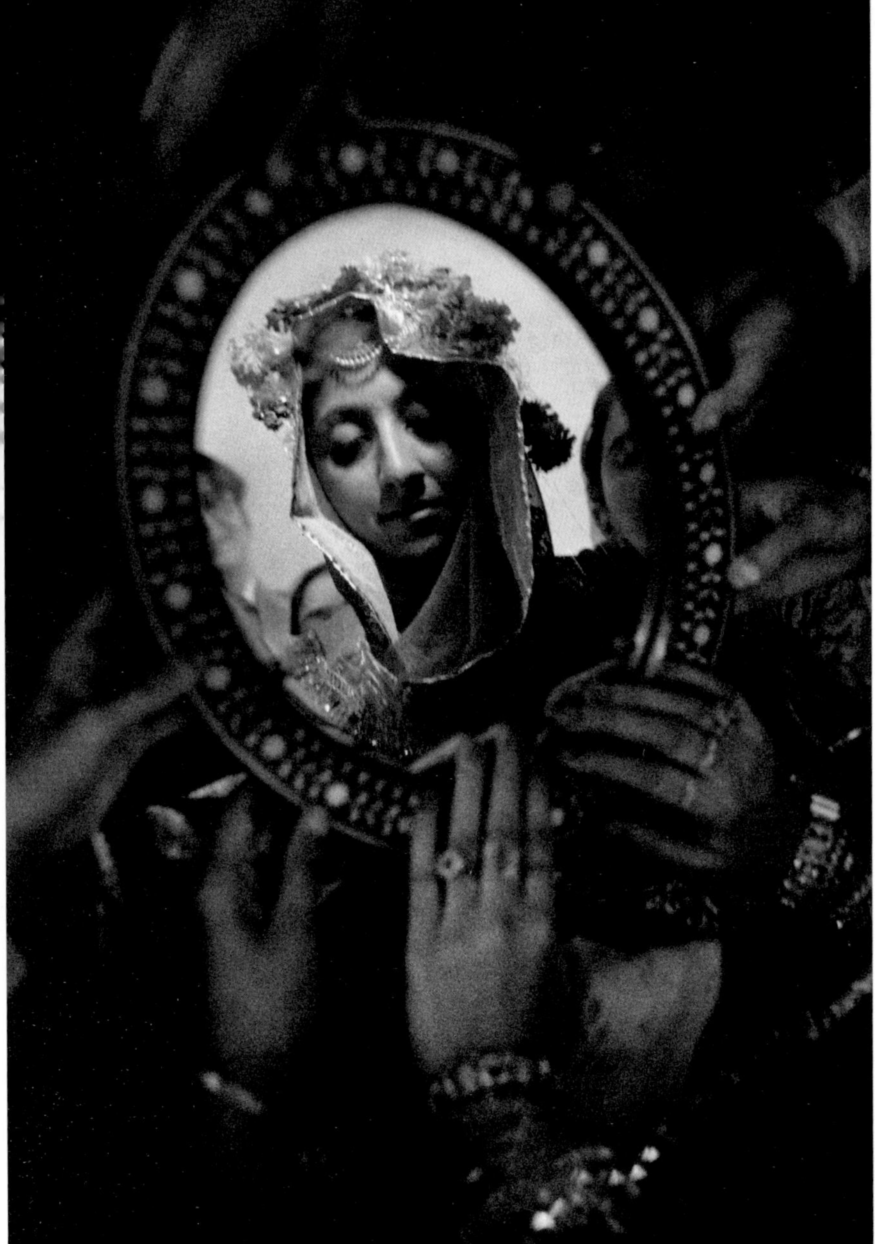

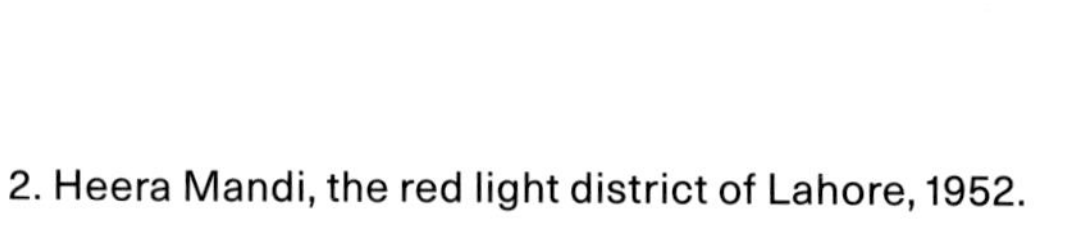
2. Heera Mandi, the red light district of Lahore, 1952.

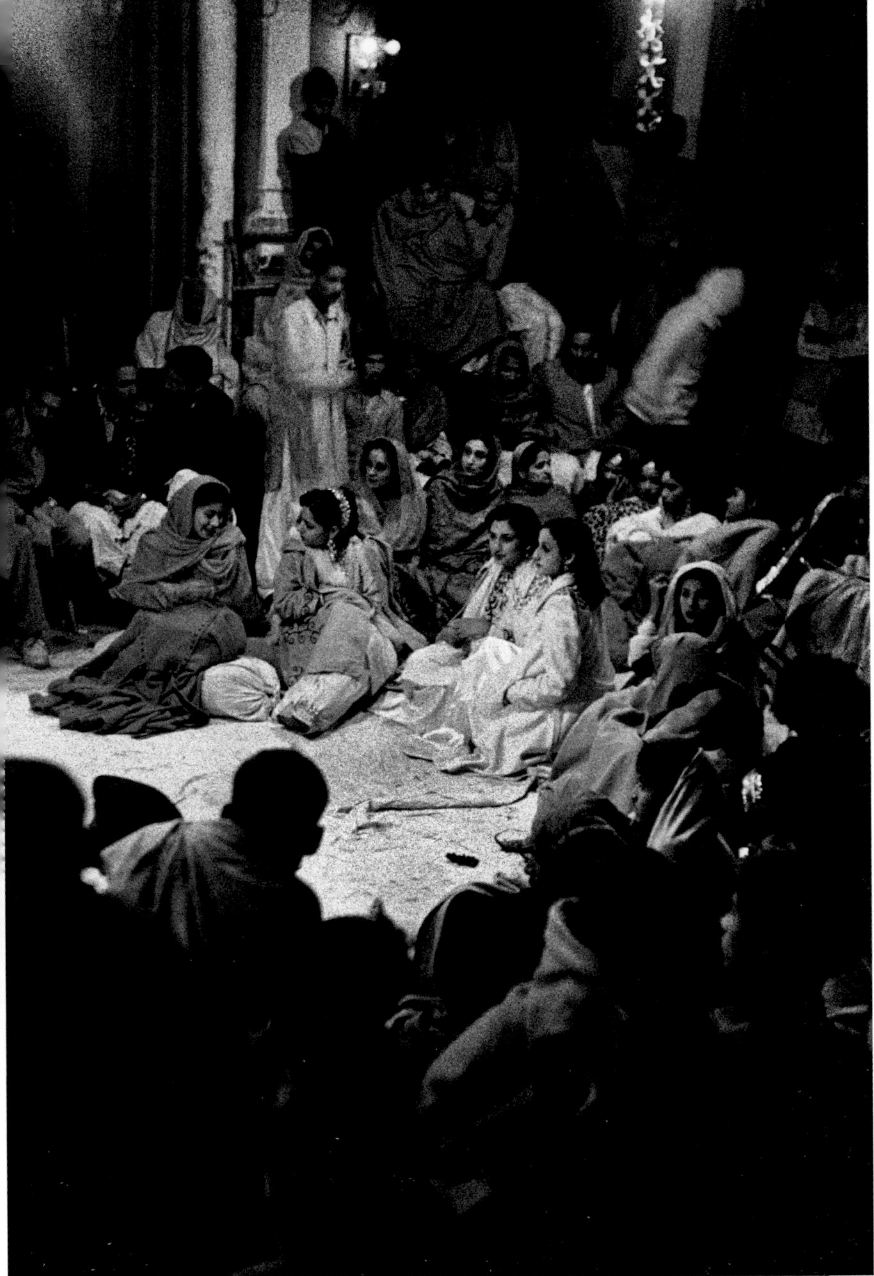

3. Heera Mandi, the red light district of Lahore, 1952.

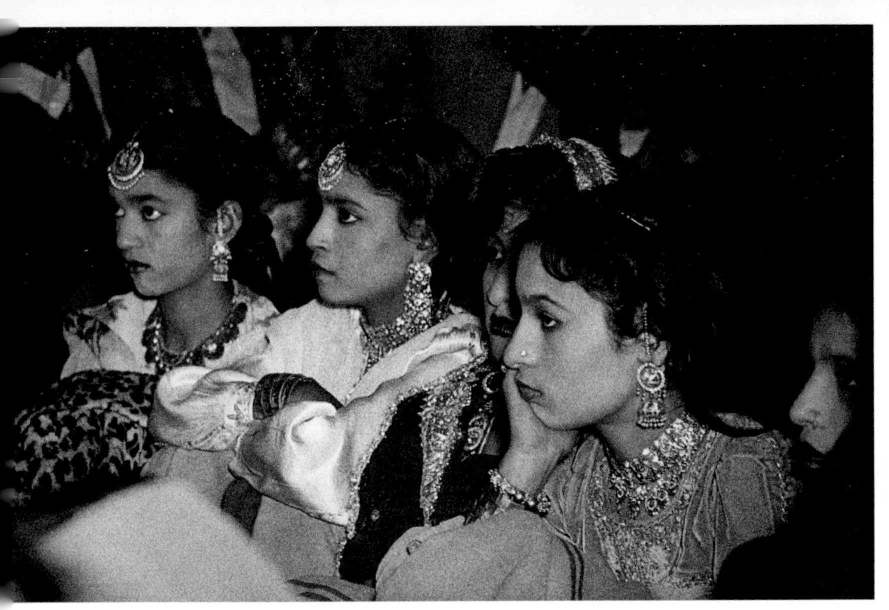

4. Lahore, 1952.

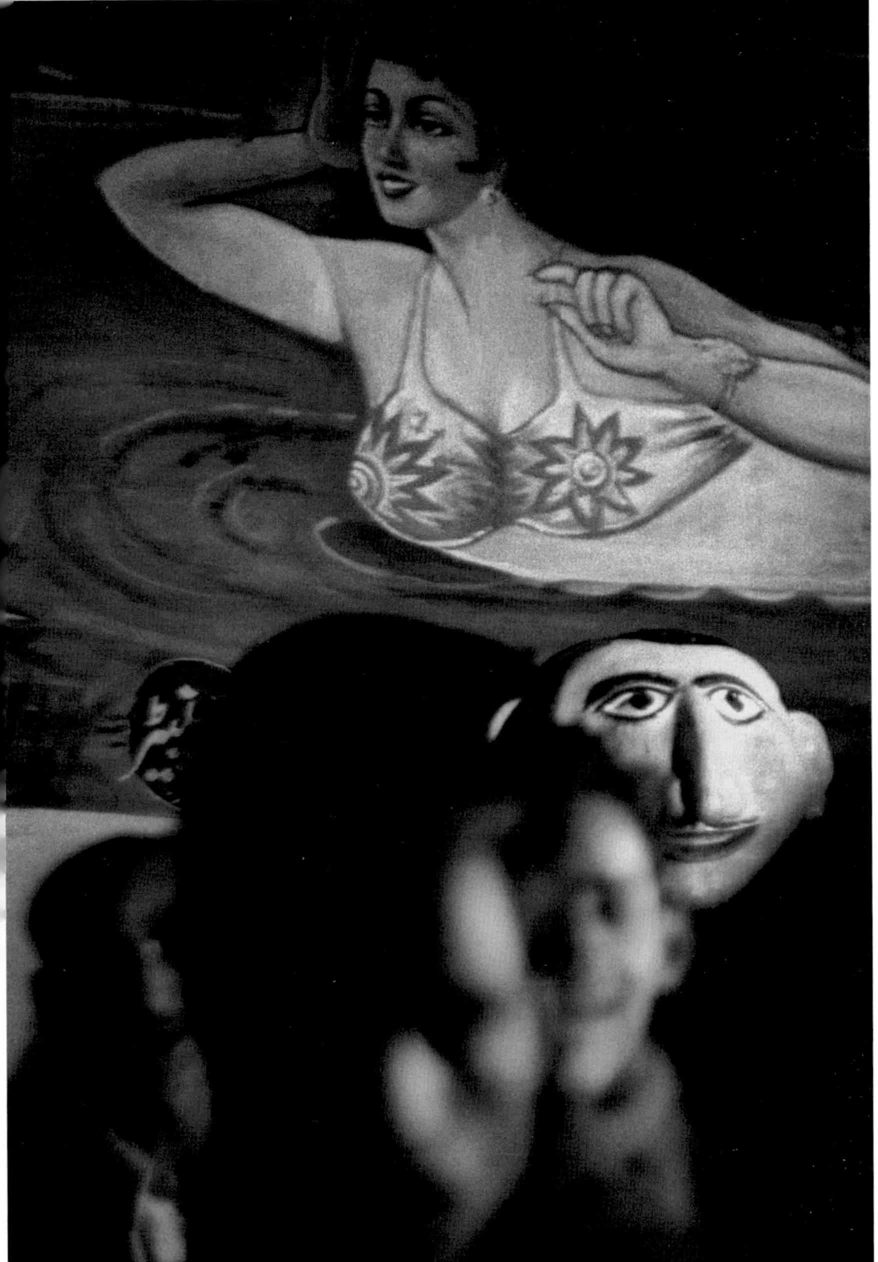

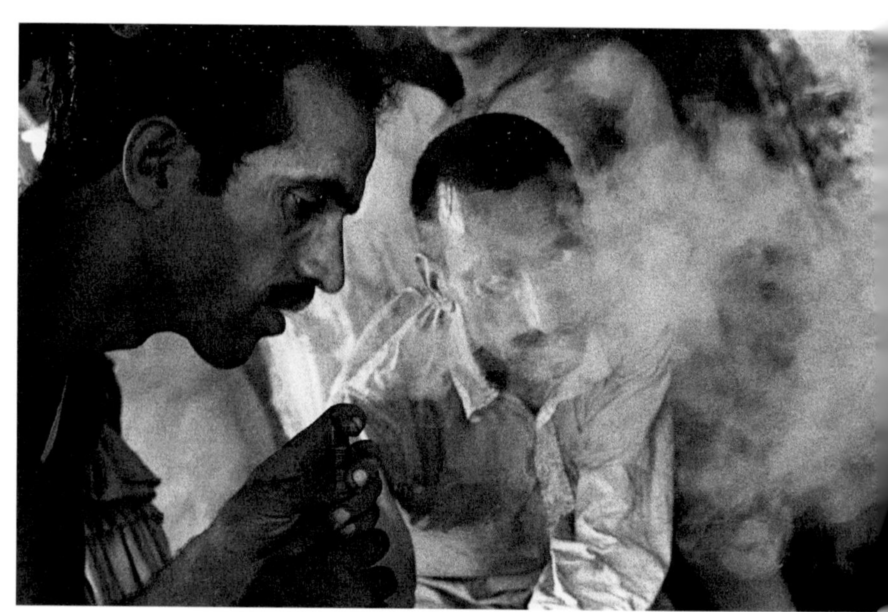

5. Hashish smokers, Lahore, 1952.

6. Samaritans celebrating Easter, near Nablus, Jordan, 1954.

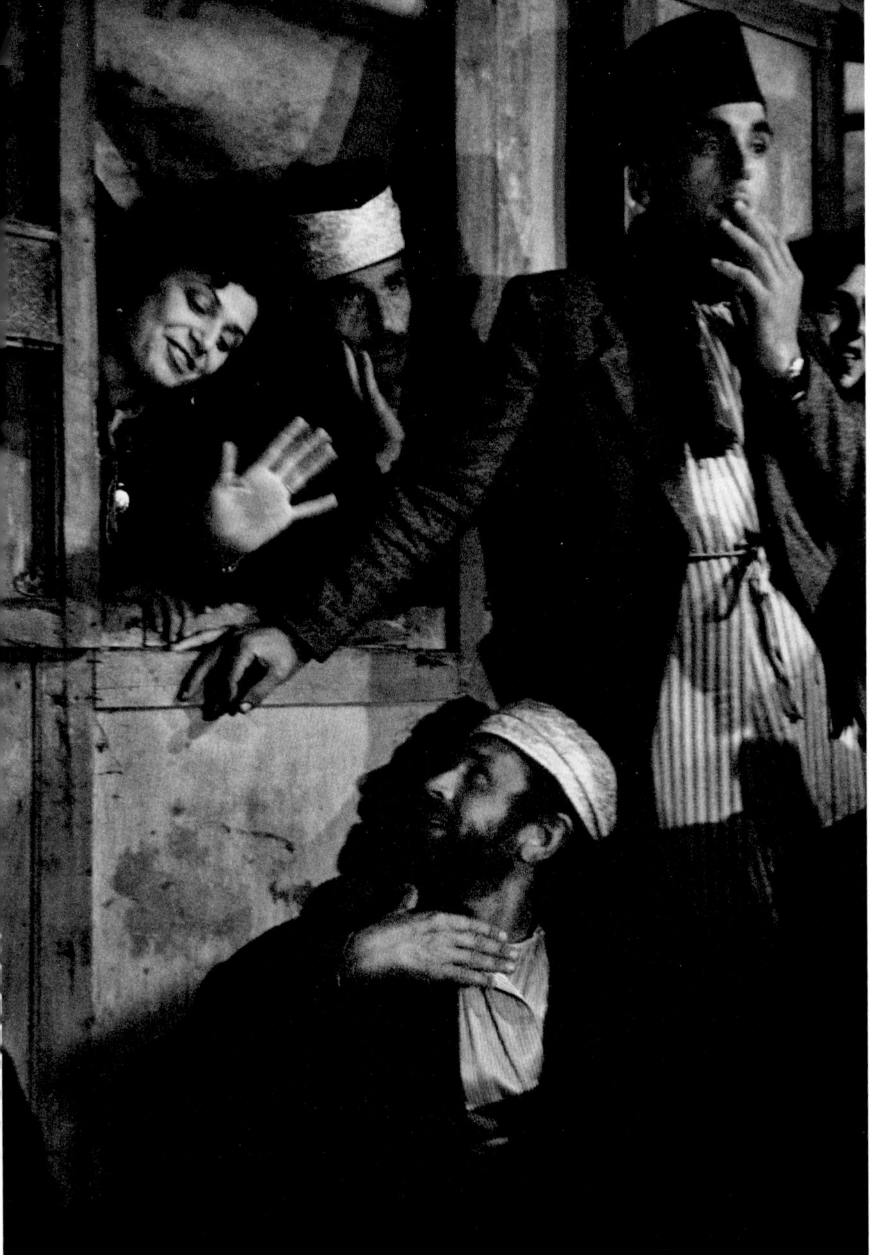

7. Lambeth, London, 1955.

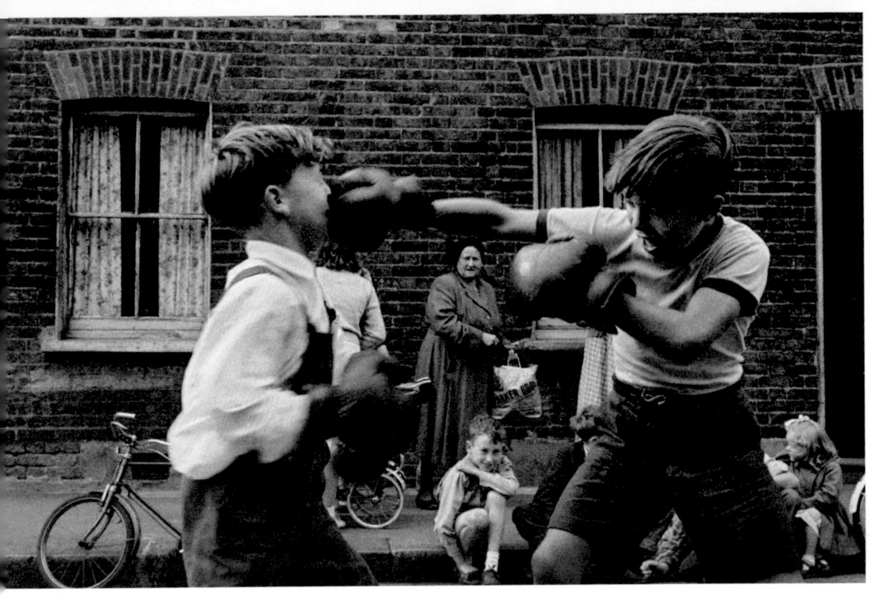

8. City of London, 1959.

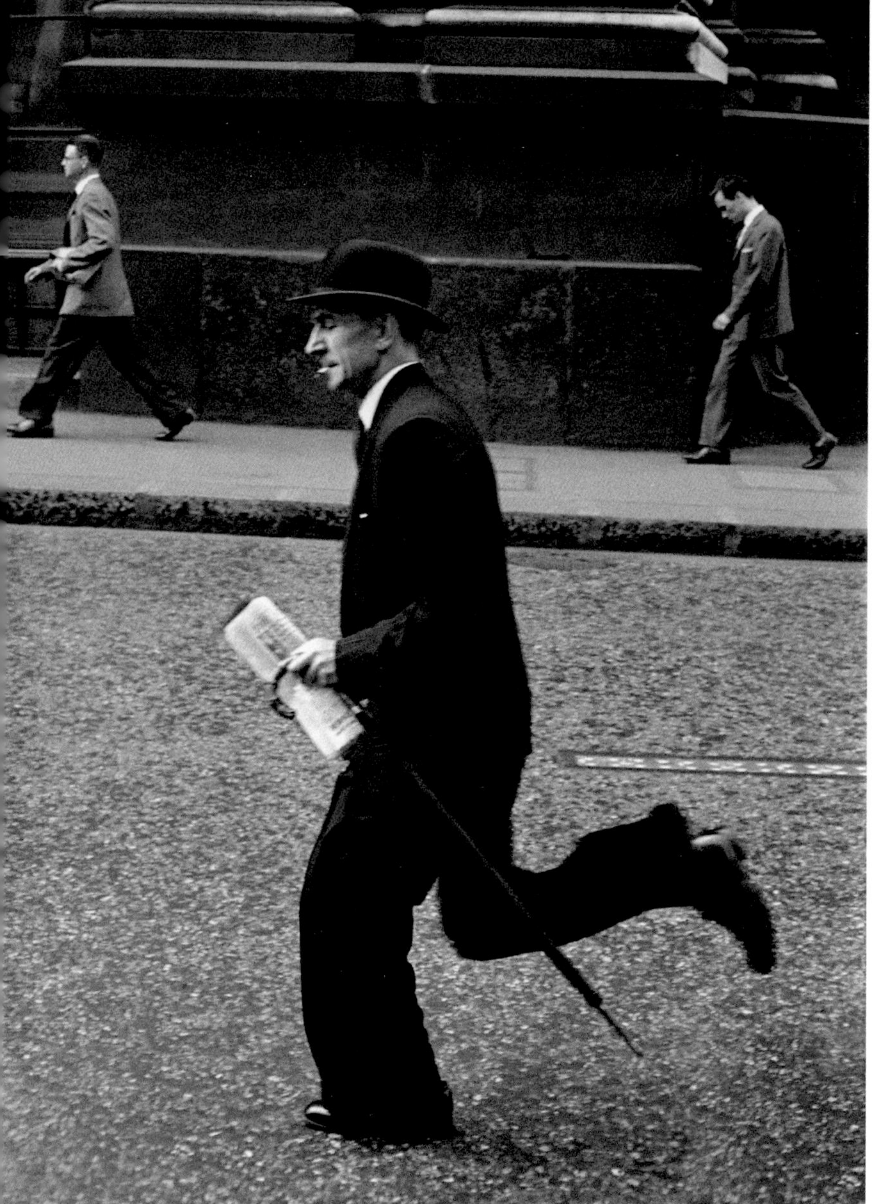

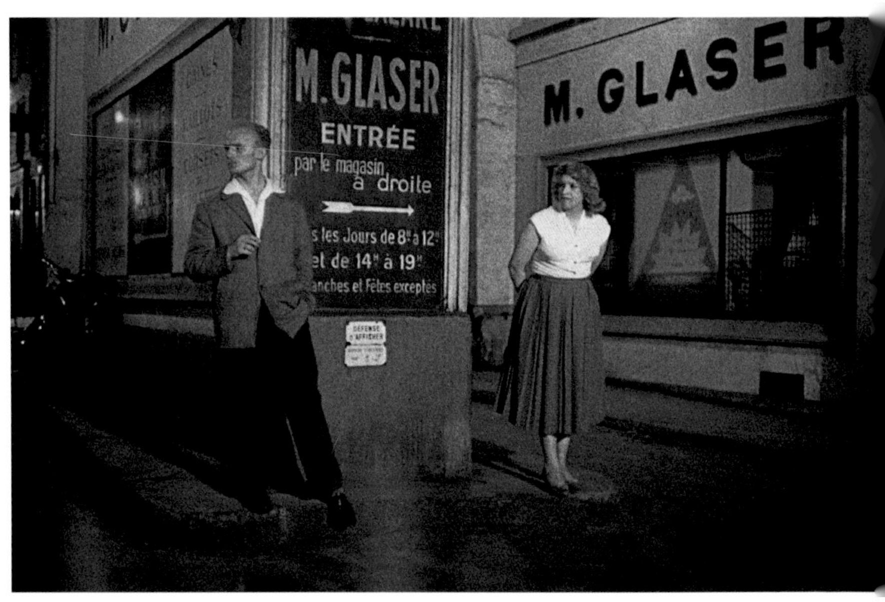

9. Prostitute, rue Saint-Denis, Paris, 1956.
10. Prostitutes, Bois de Boulogne, Paris, 1956.

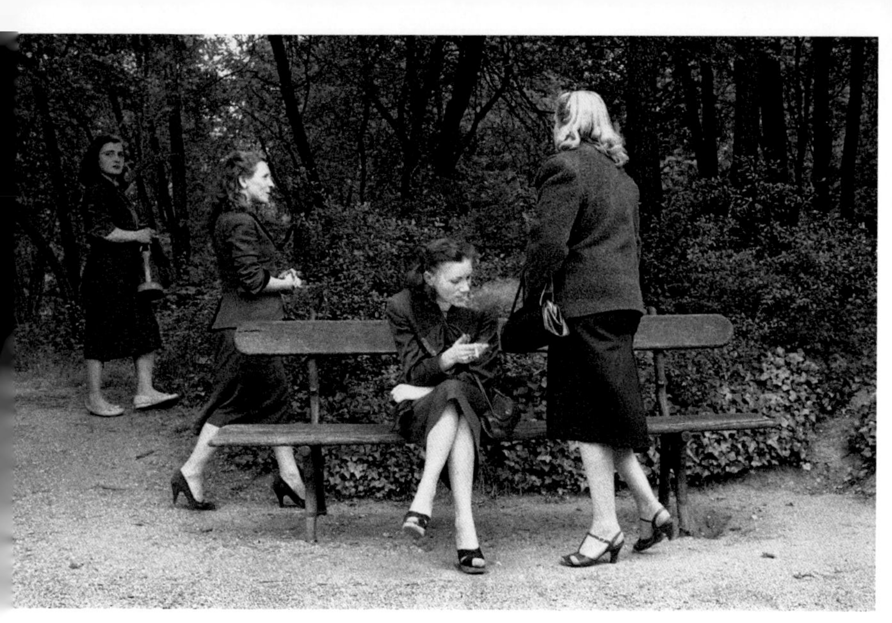

11. Bar in Pigalle, Paris, 1956.

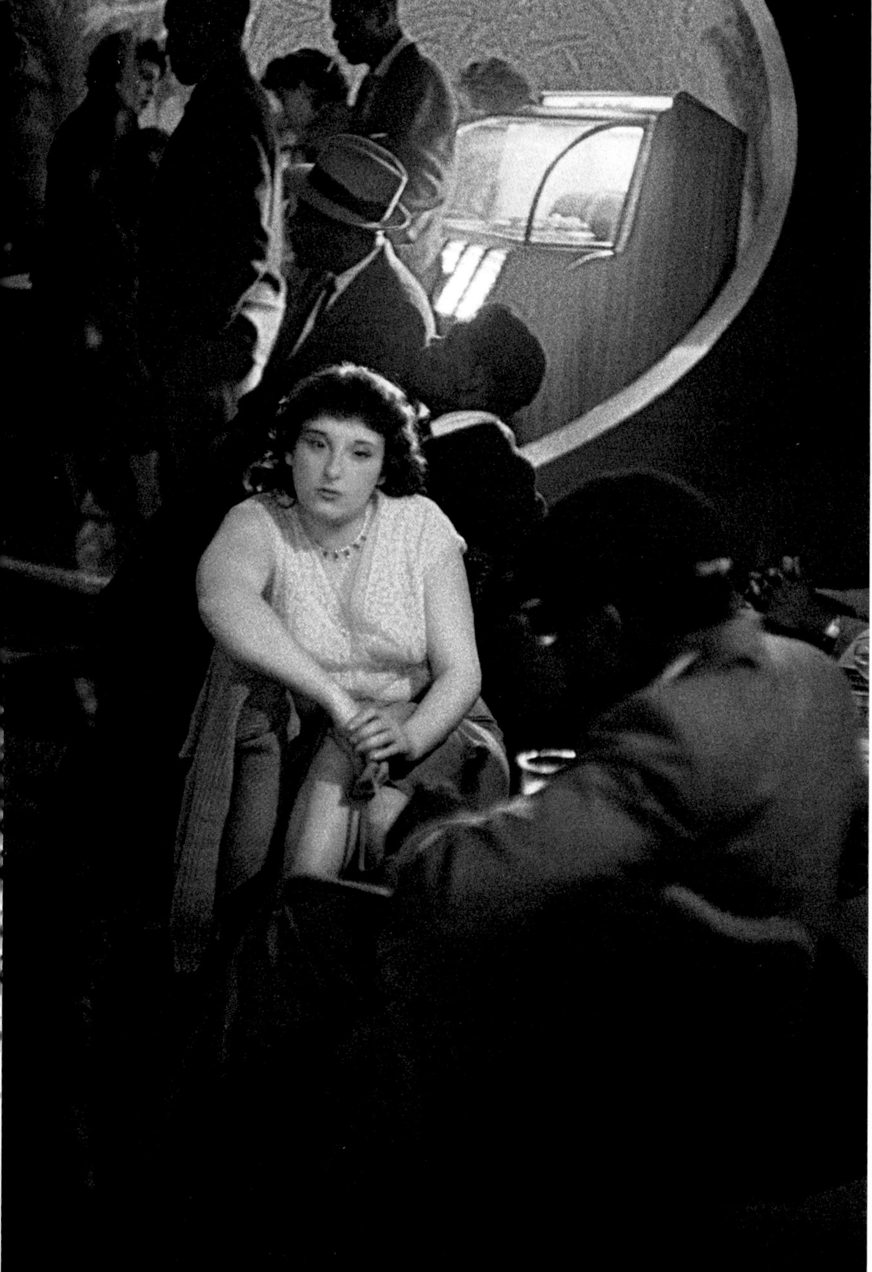

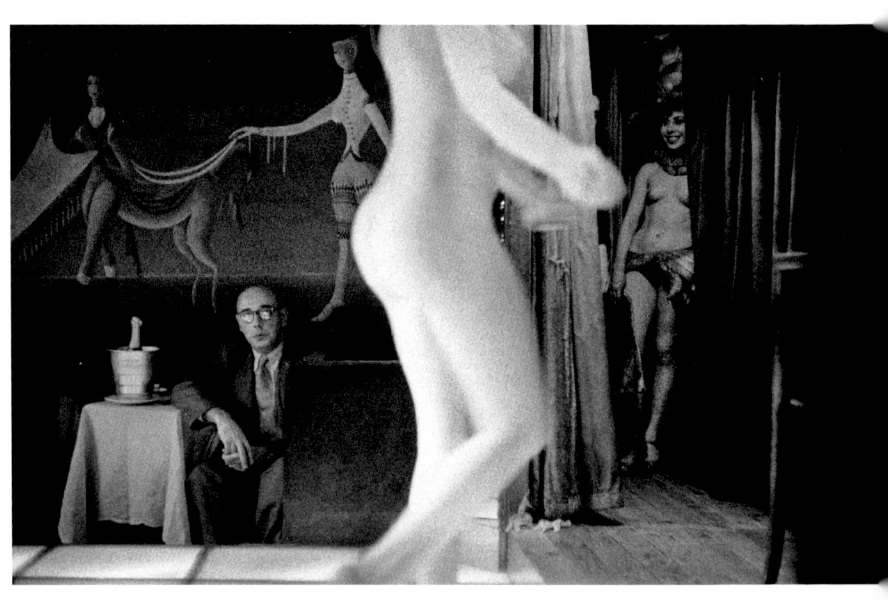

12–13. Cabaret Le Sphinx in Pigalle, Paris, 1956.

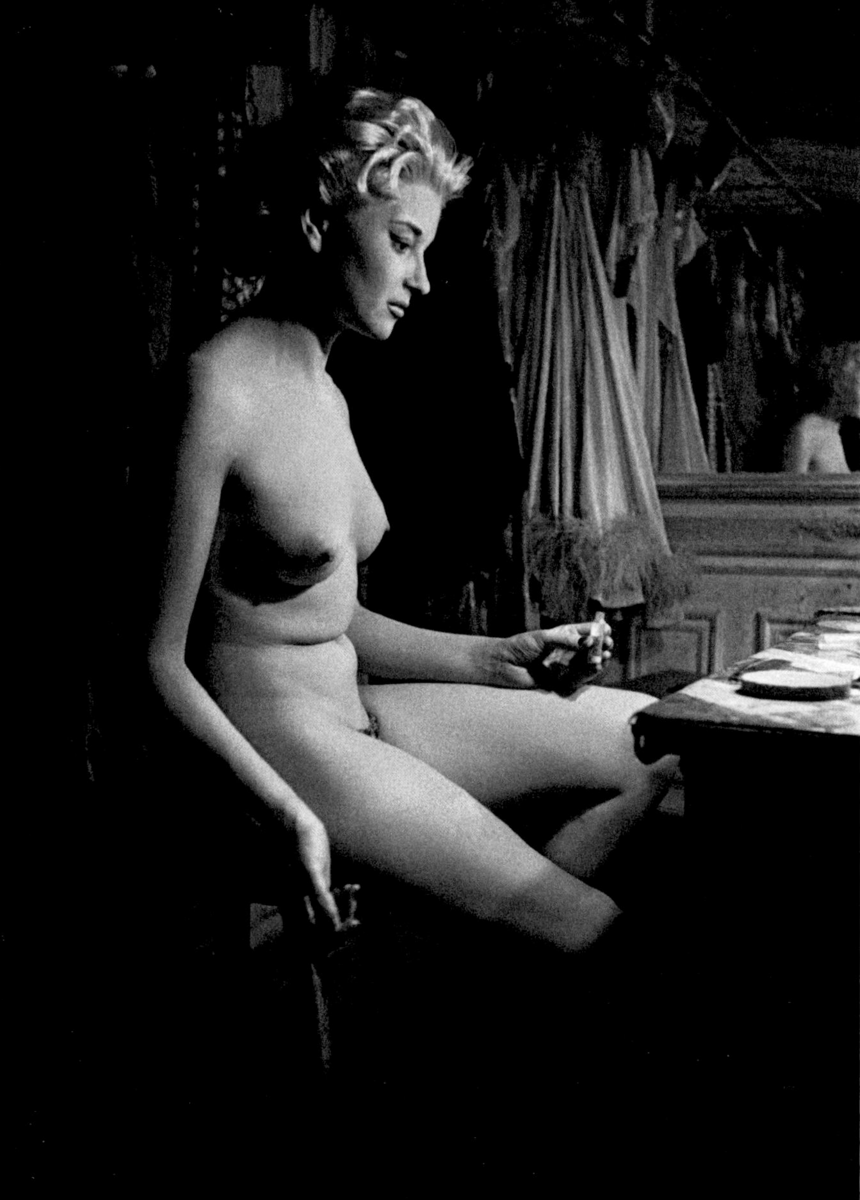

14. Self-portrait, Cabaret Le Sphinx in Pigalle, Paris, 1956.

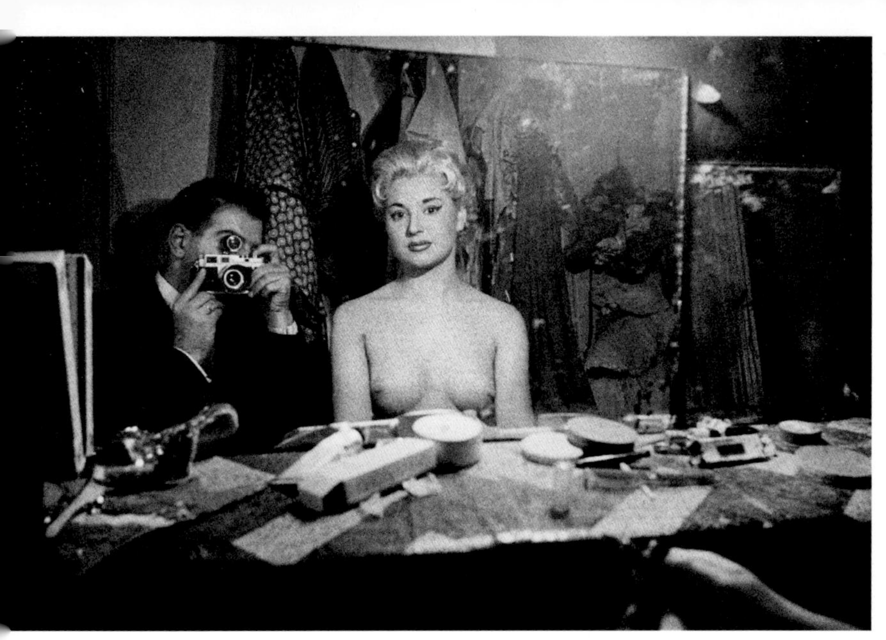

15. Cabaret Le Sphinx in Pigalle, Paris, 1956.

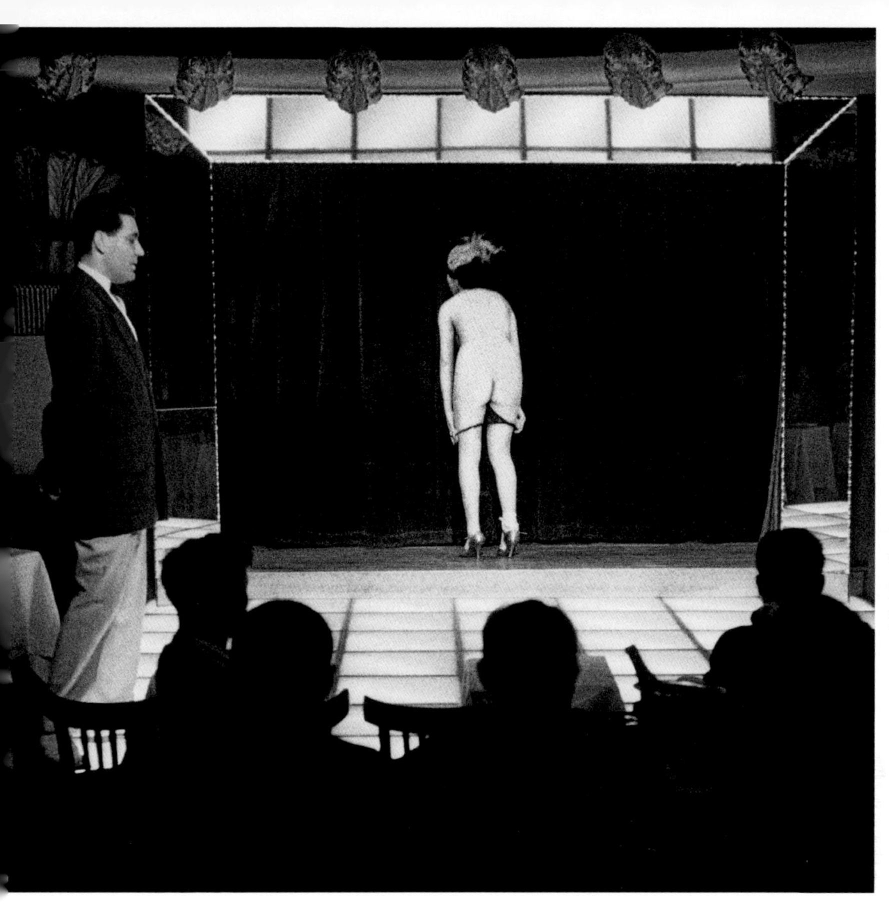

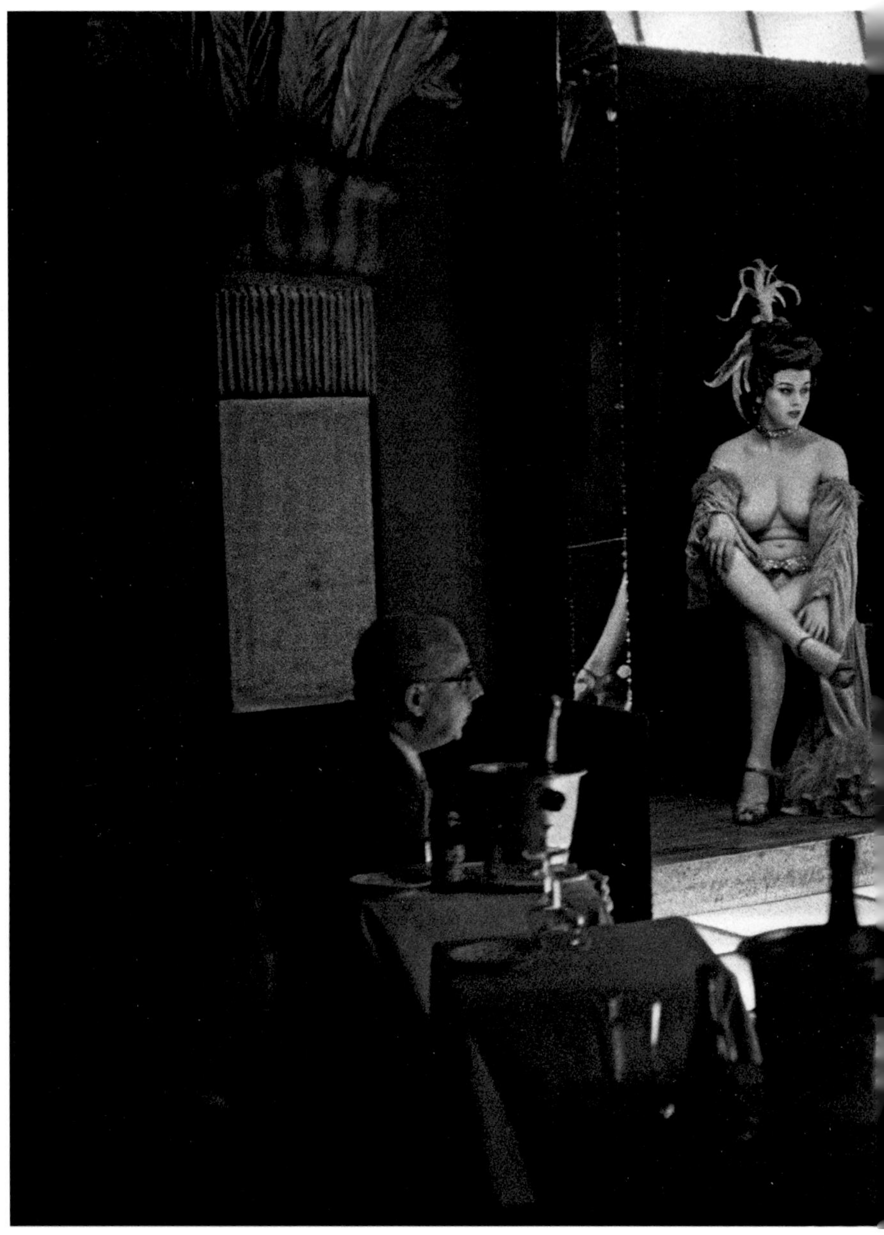

16. Cabaret Le Sphinx in Pigalle, Paris, 1956.

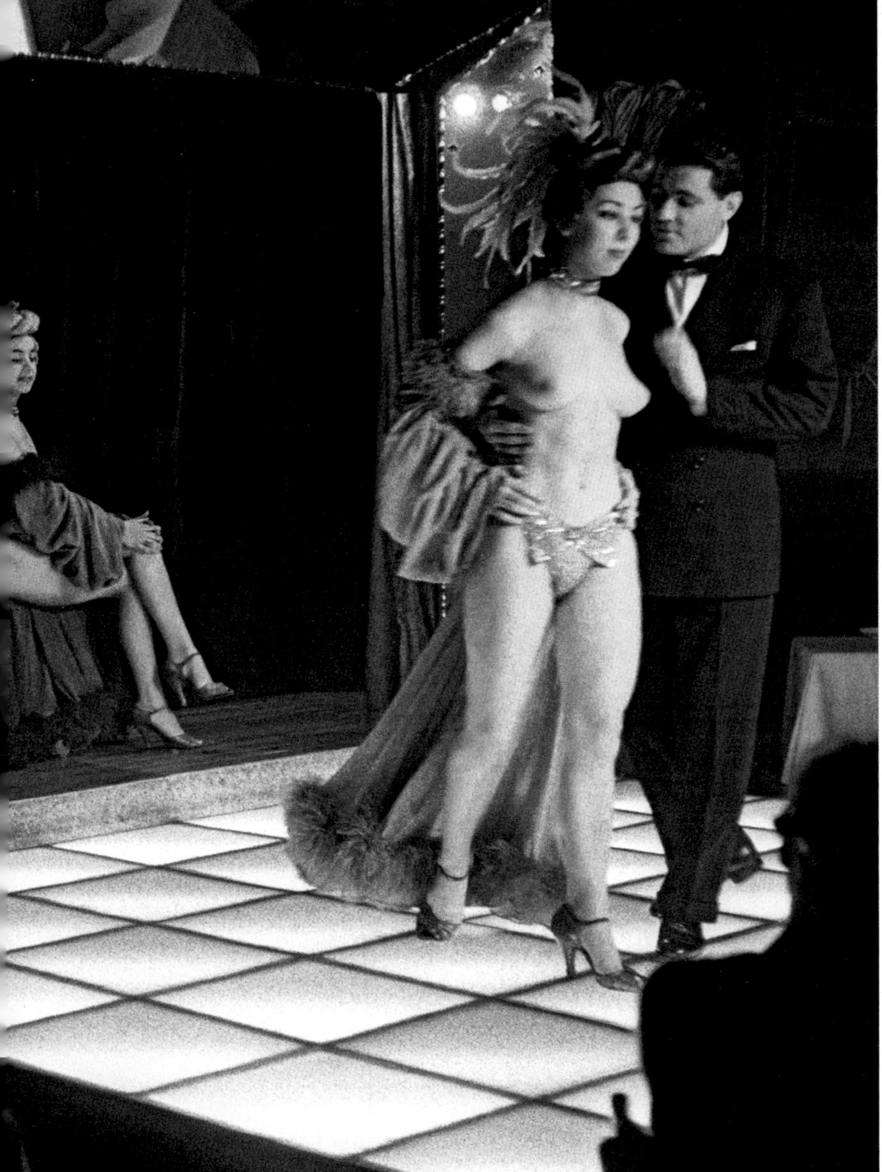

17. Soho, London, 1959.

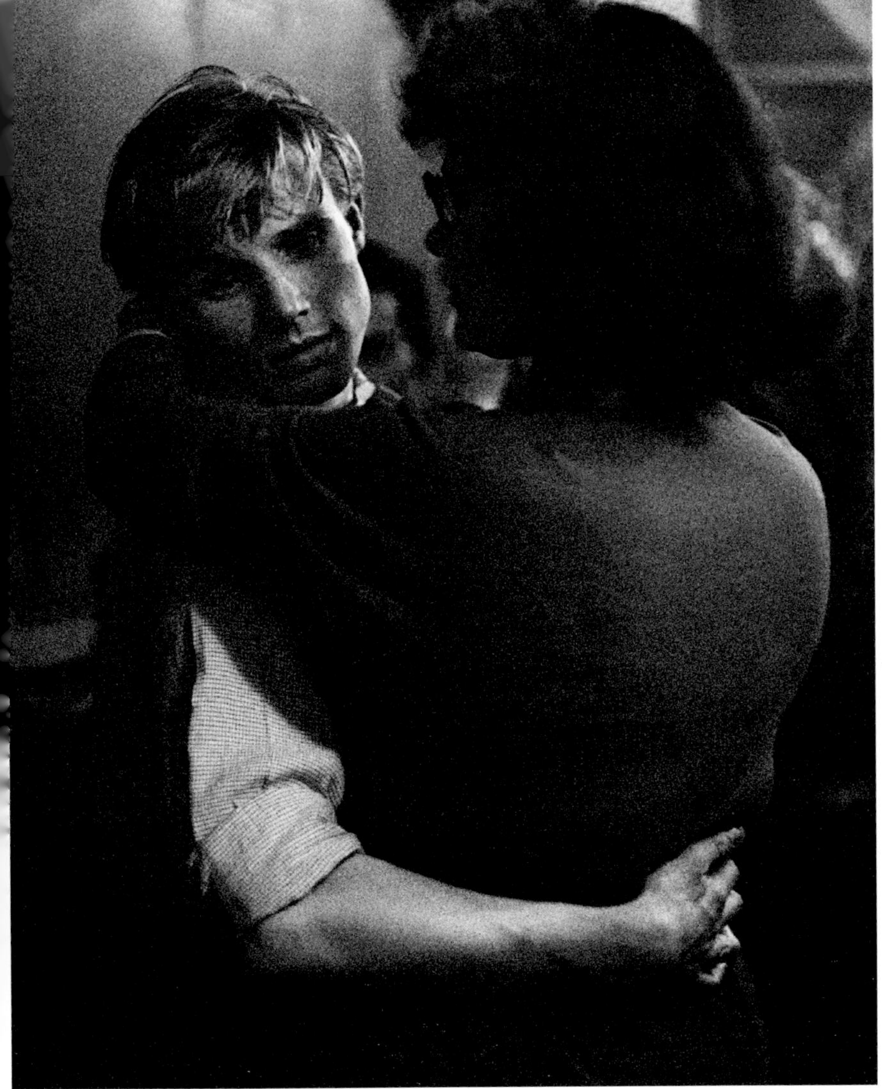

18. Lido, Paris, 1956.

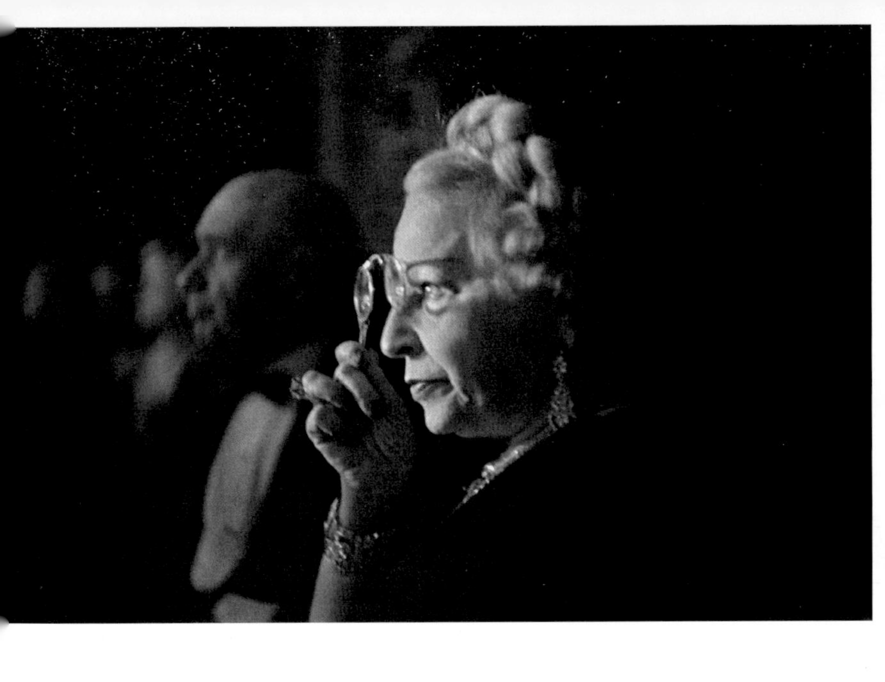

19. Coco Chanel hiding on a staircase to watch
her fashion show, rue Cambon, Paris, 1958.

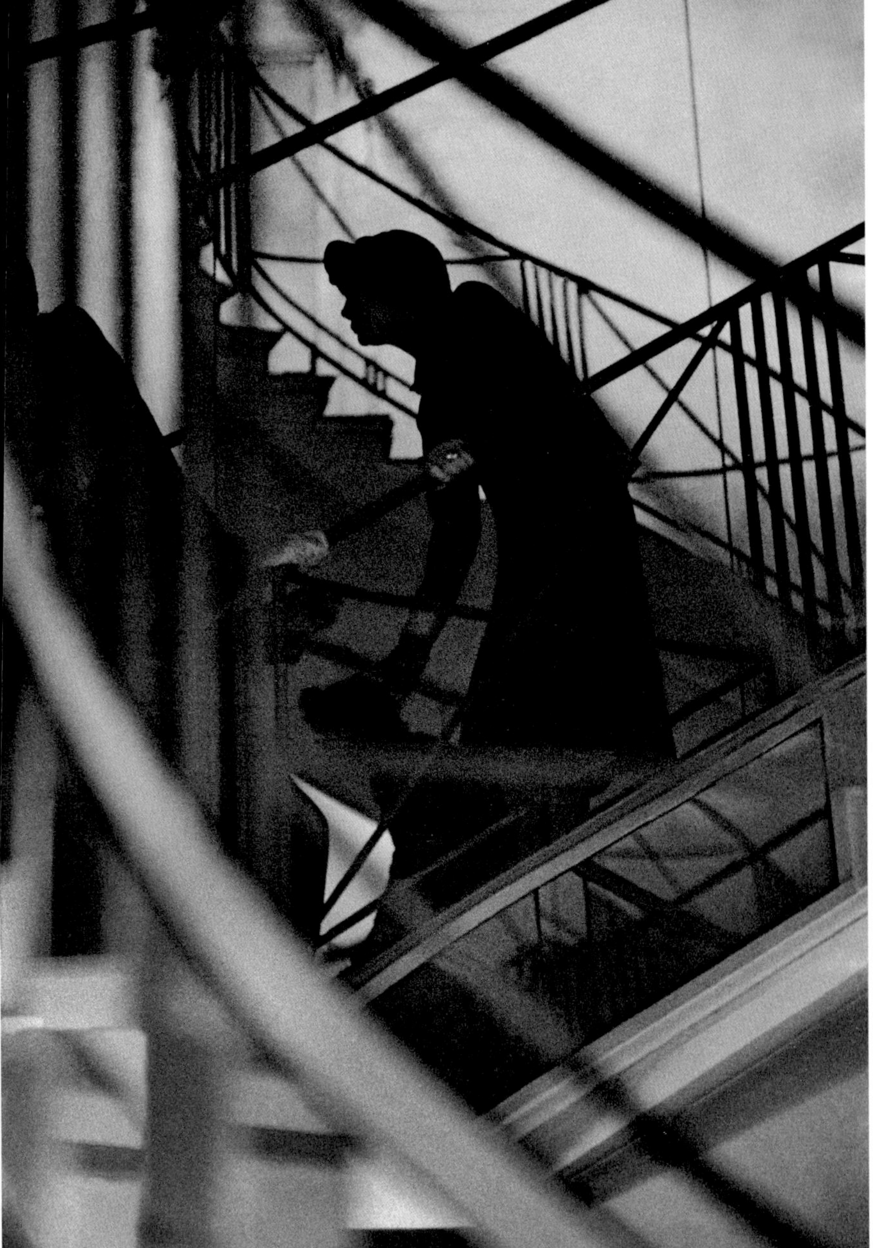

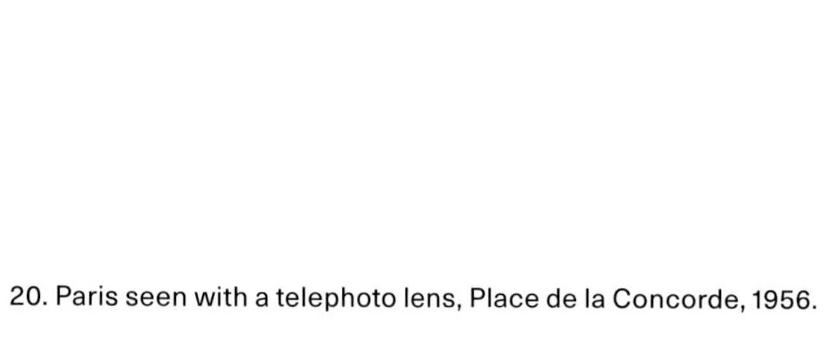

20. Paris seen with a telephoto lens, Place de la Concorde, 1956.

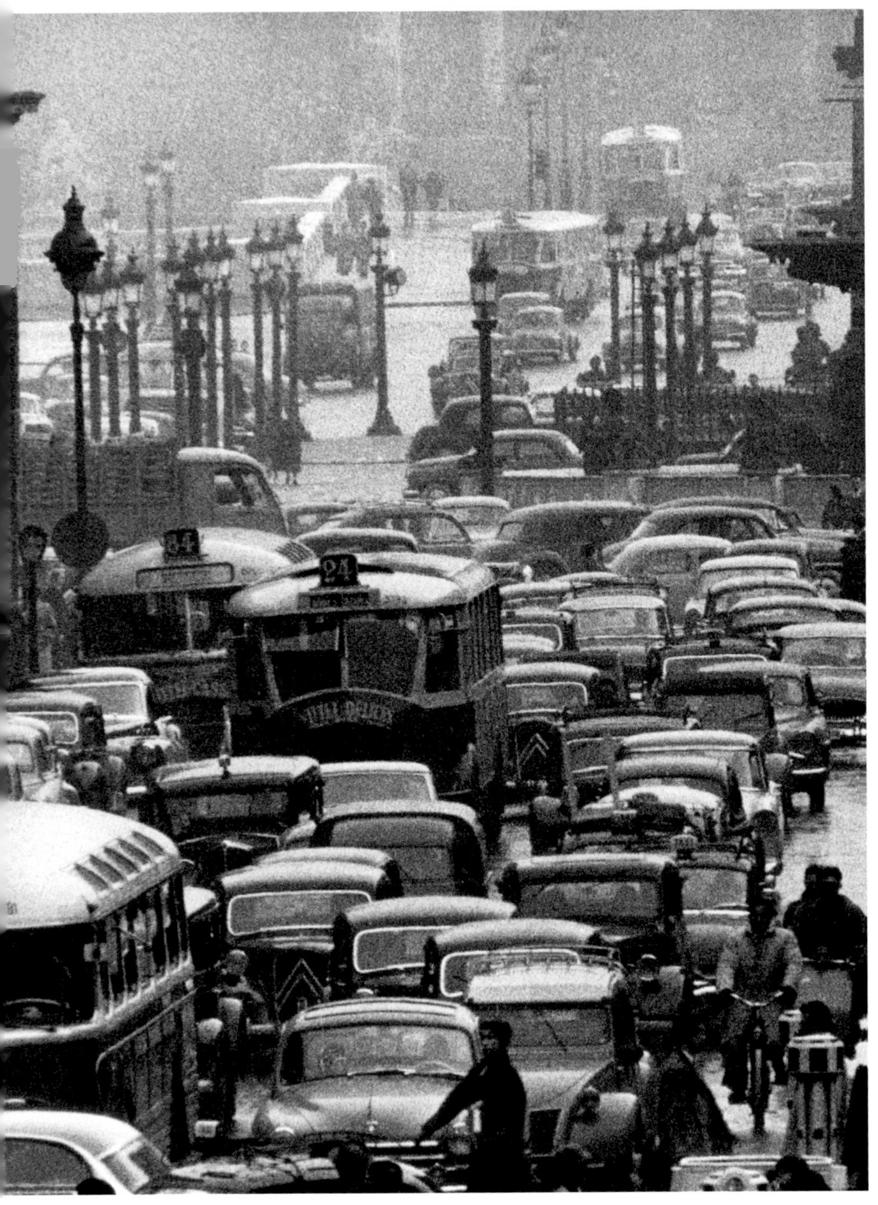

21. Paris, 1955.

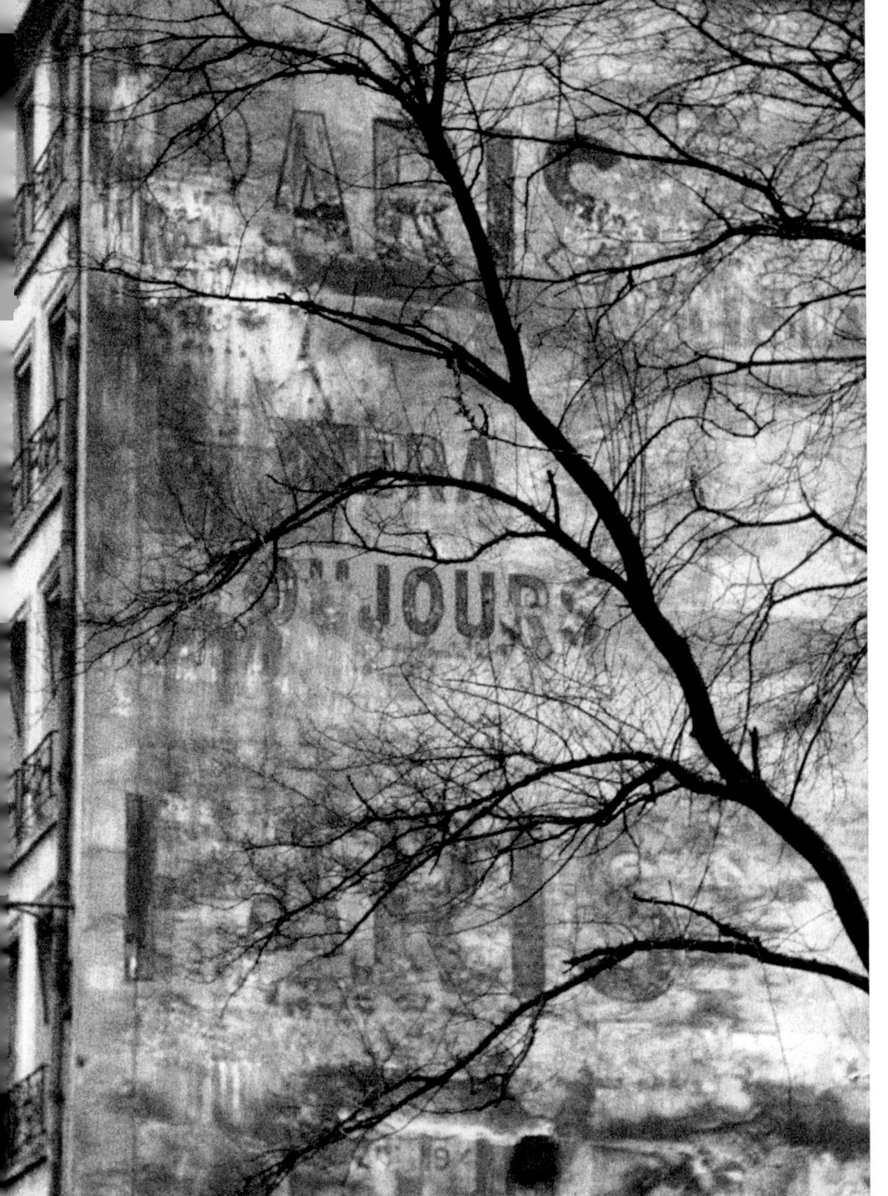

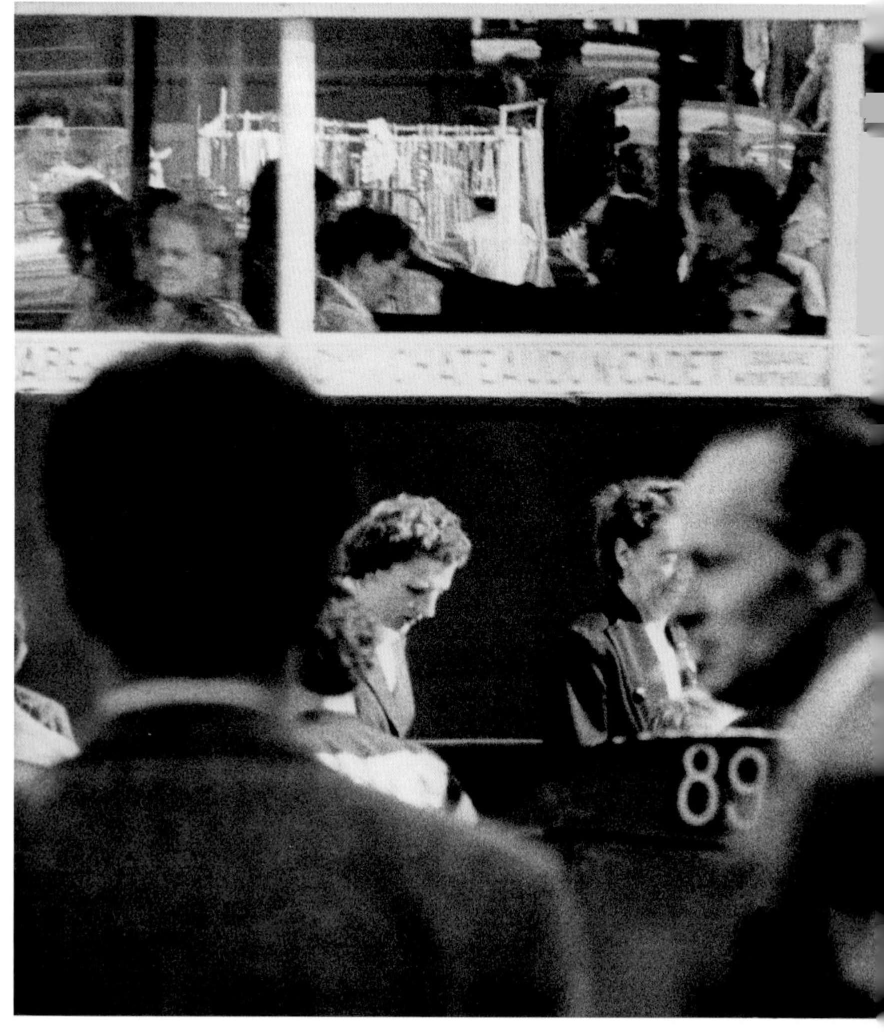

22. Paris seen with a telephoto lens, 1956.

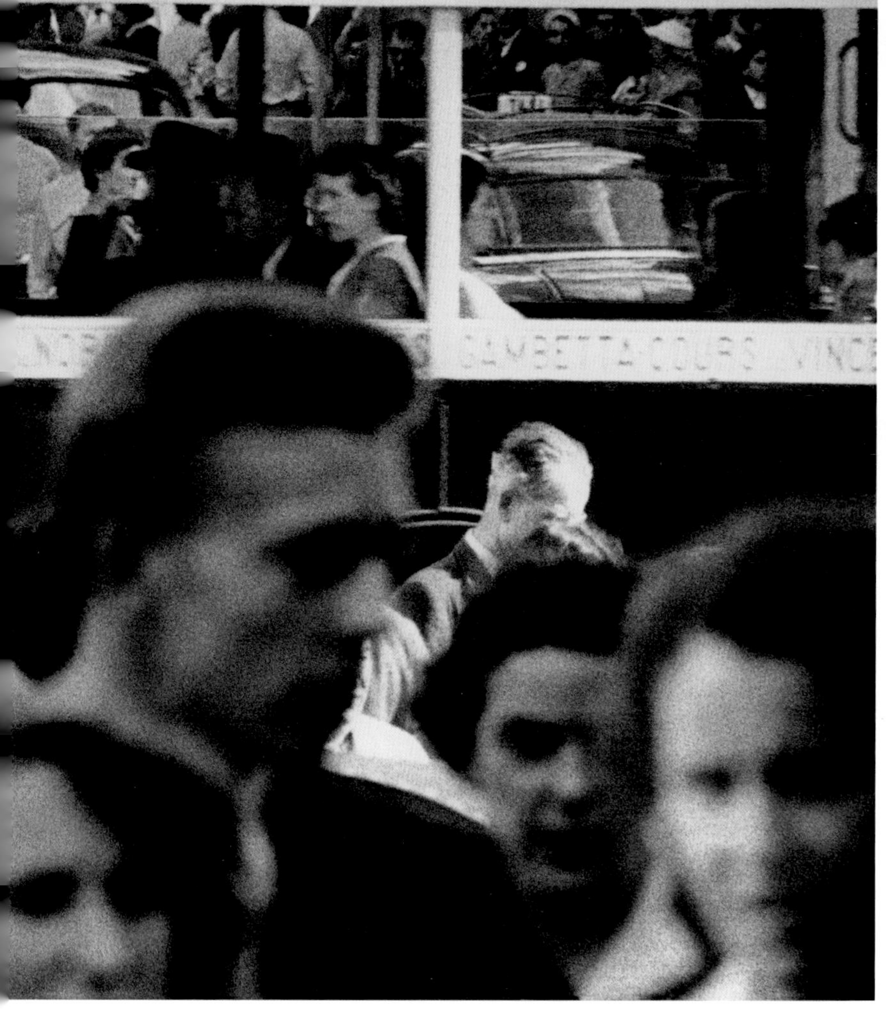
GAMBETTA COURS VINC

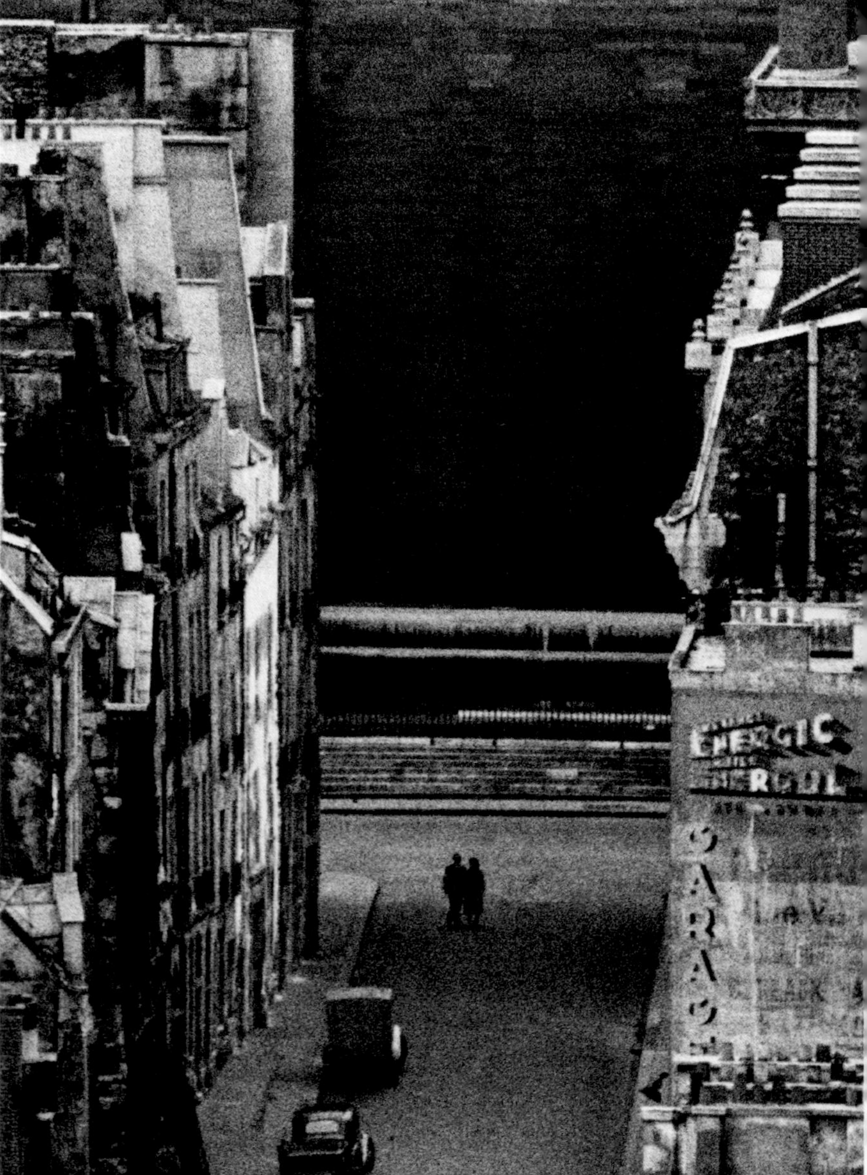
ENERGIC
ENERGOL
GARAGE

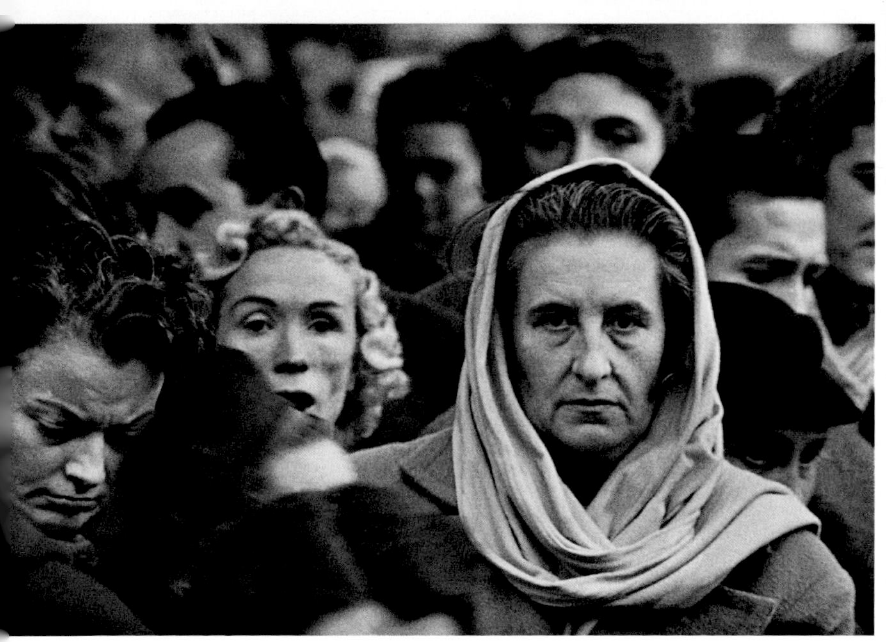

23. Paris seen with a telephoto lens, wall of
the Panthéon from Notre Dame, 1956.
24. Paris seen with a telephoto lens,
Galeries Lafayette, Paris, 1956.

25. Gare Saint-Lazare, Paris, 1959.

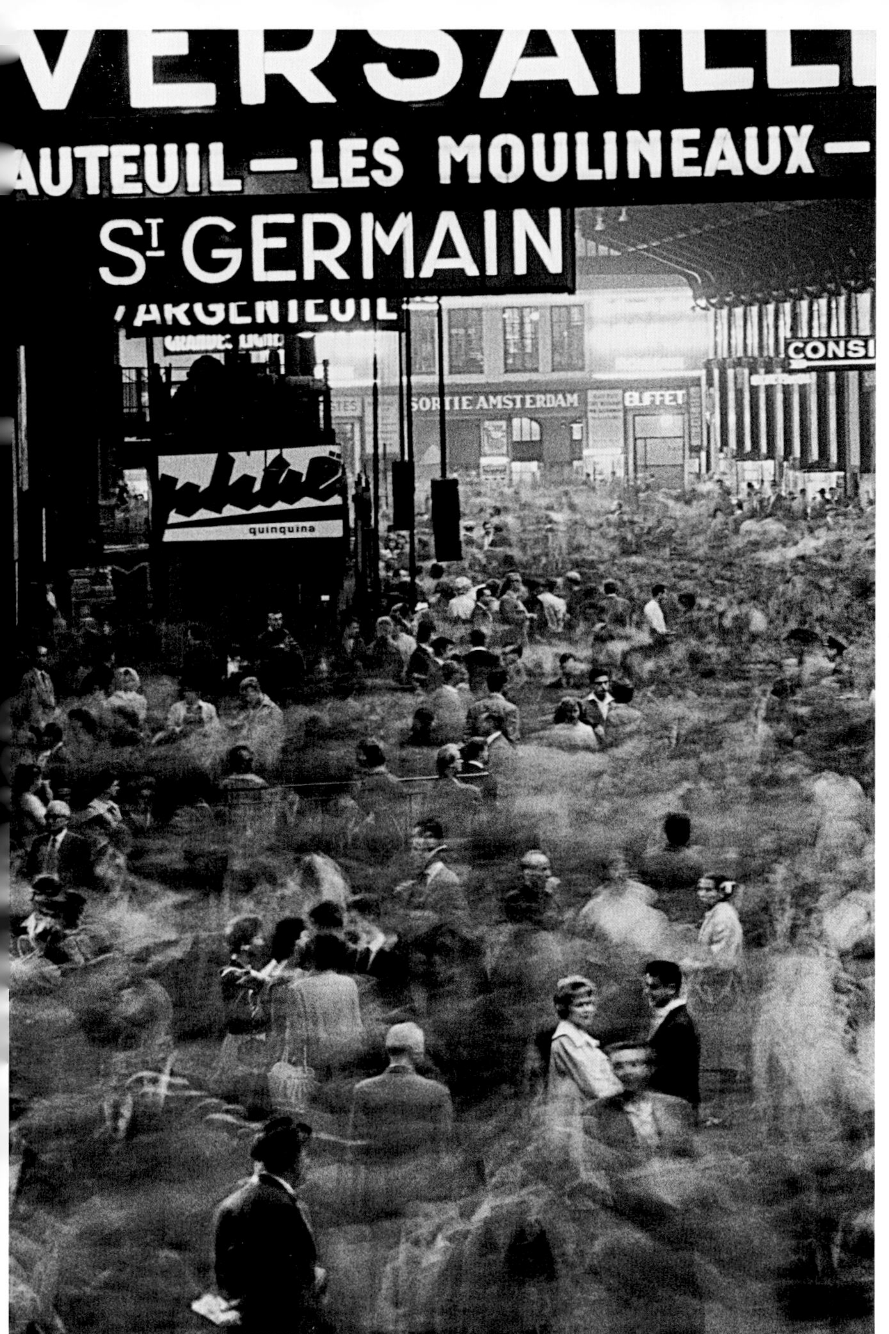

VERSAILL
AUTEUIL — LES MOULINEAUX —
St GERMAIN
ARGENTEUIL
SORTIE AMSTERDAM
BUFFET
CONS
quinquina

26. Anna Karina in Les Halles, for *Jours de France*, Paris, 1959.

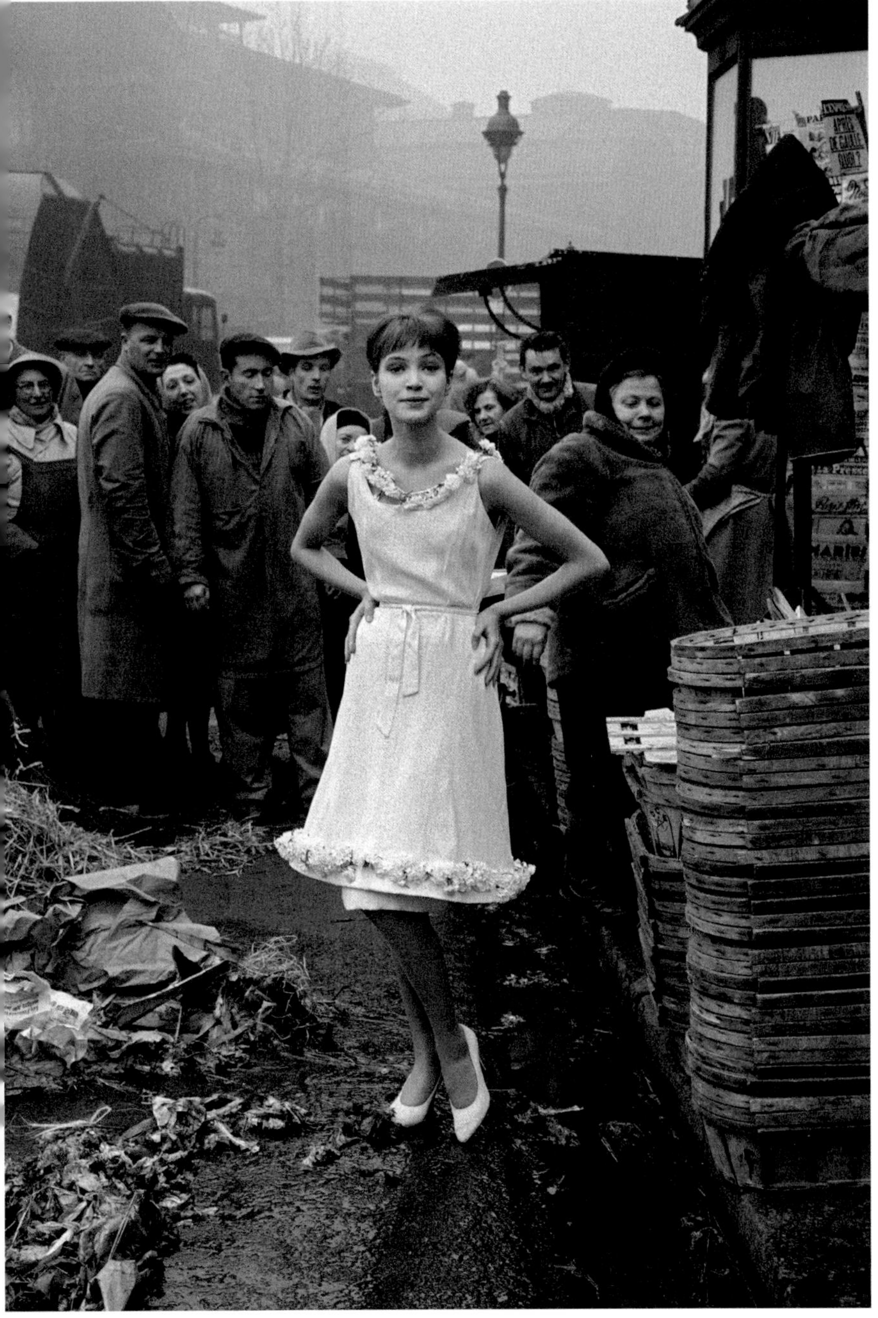

27. Tan Arnold at the Chien qui Fume, for *Jardin des Modes*, Paris, 1957.

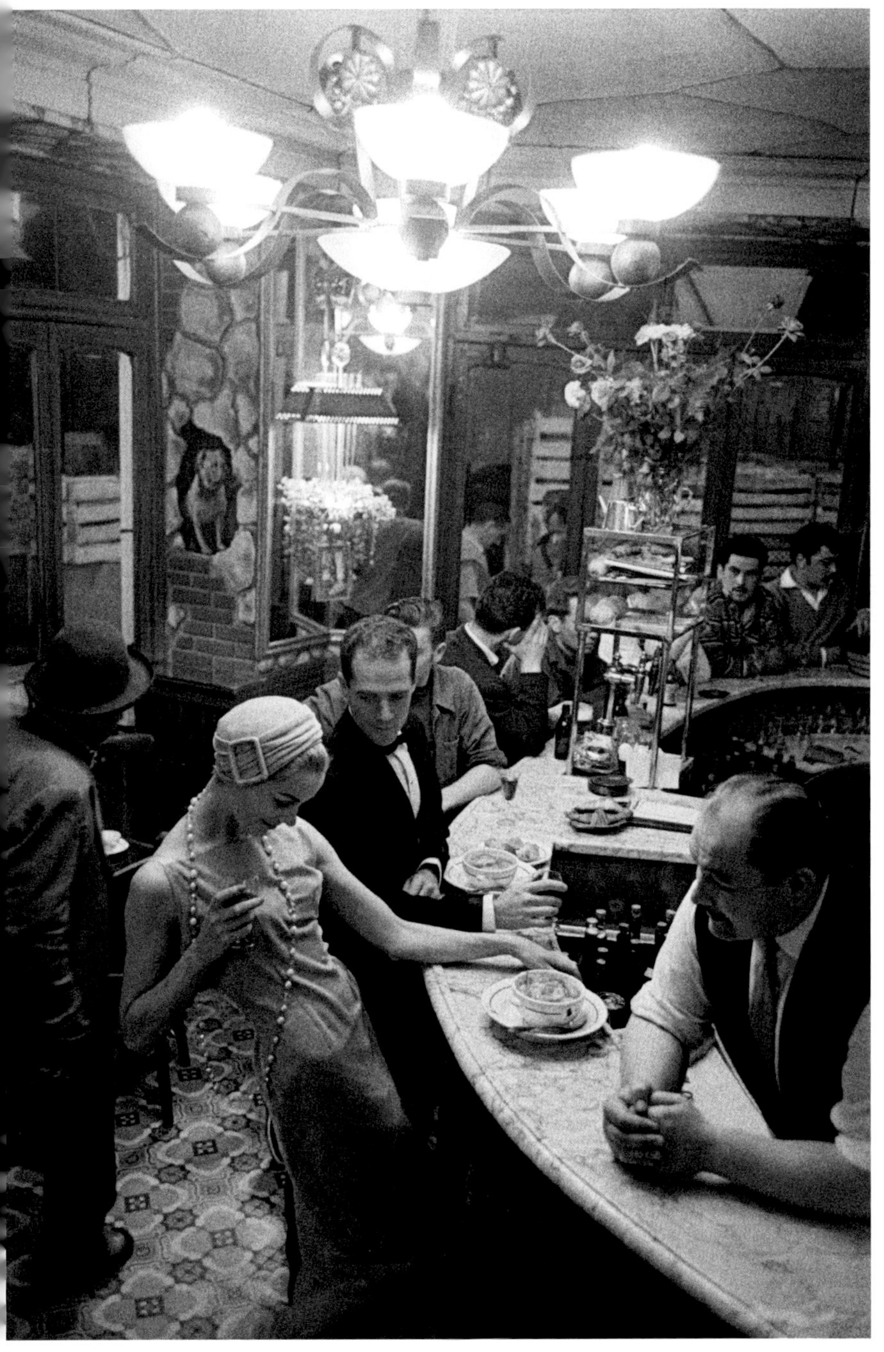

28. For *Vogue* UK, Paris, 1961.

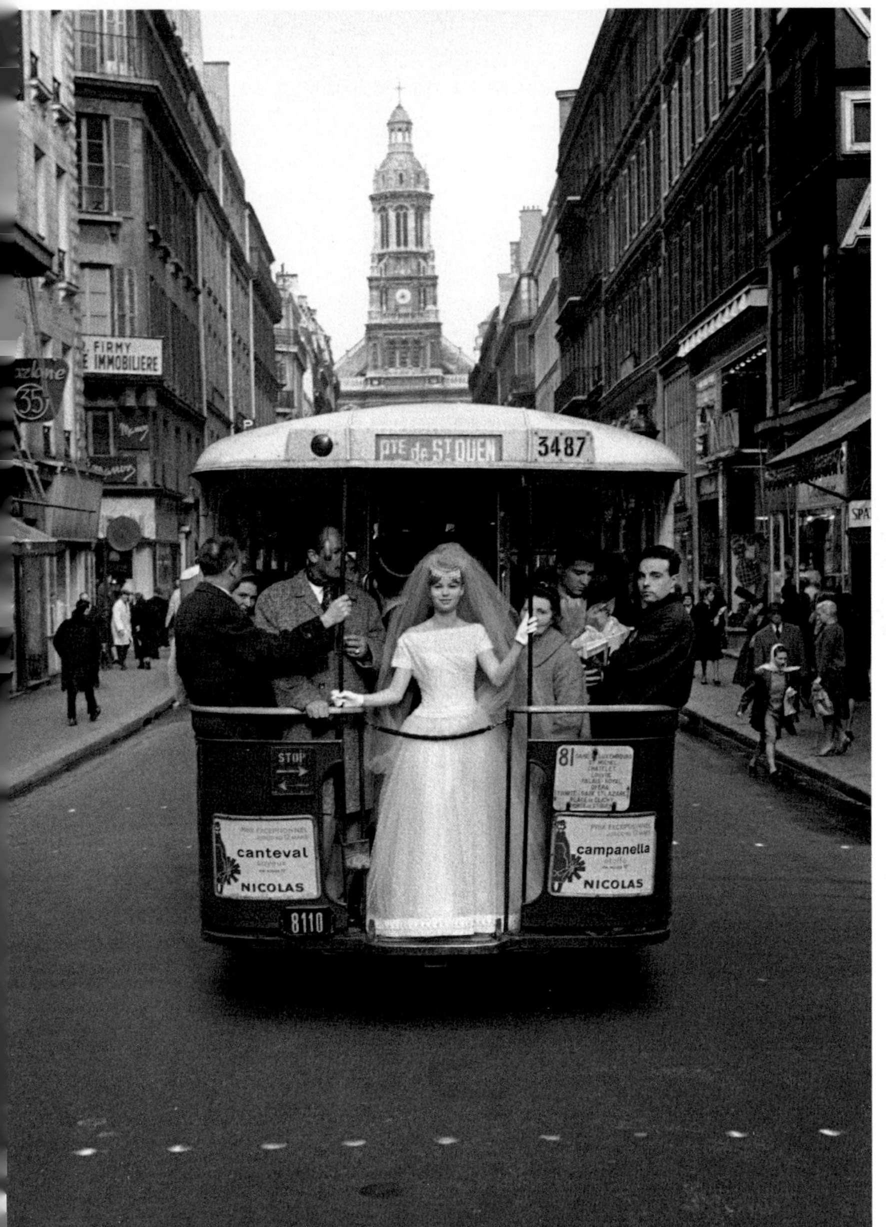
FIRMY
IMMOBILIERE
35
PTE de ST OUEN
3487
STOP
81
canteval
NICOLAS
8110
campanella
NICOLAS

29. Givenchy, for *Jardin des Modes*, Paris, 1958.

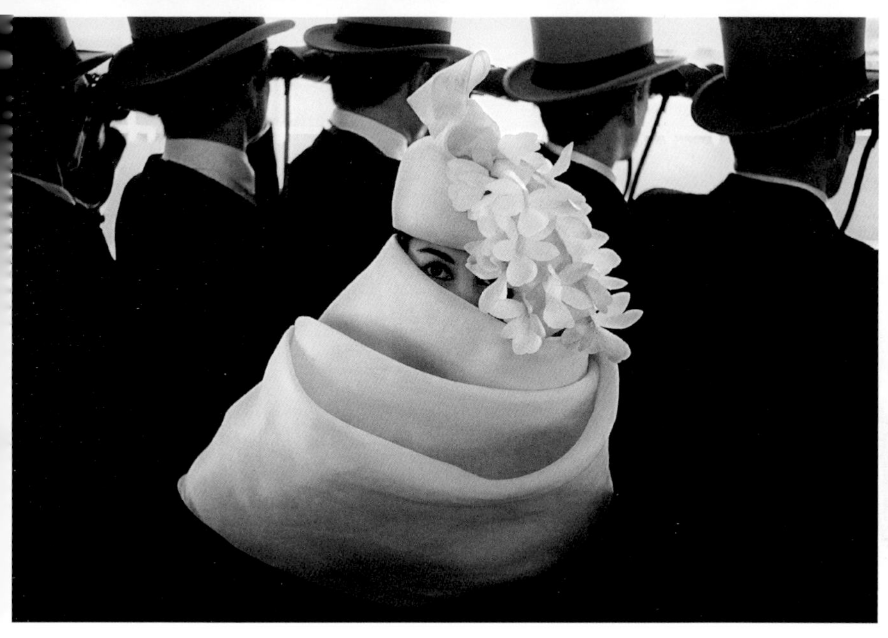

30. Monique Dutto at the Metro exit,
for *Jours de France*, Paris, 1959.

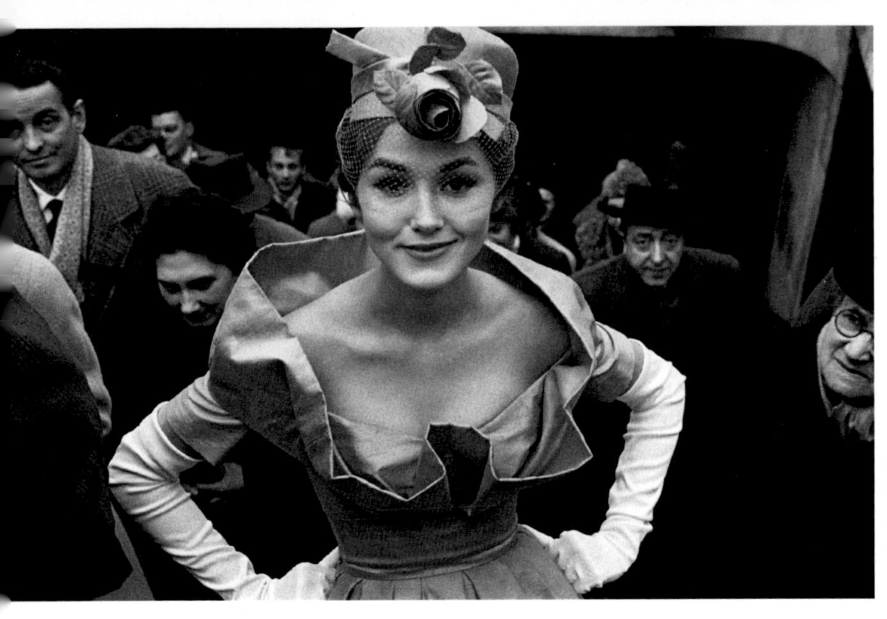

31. Carol Lobravico at the Café de Flore,
for *Harper's Bazaar*, Paris, 1962.

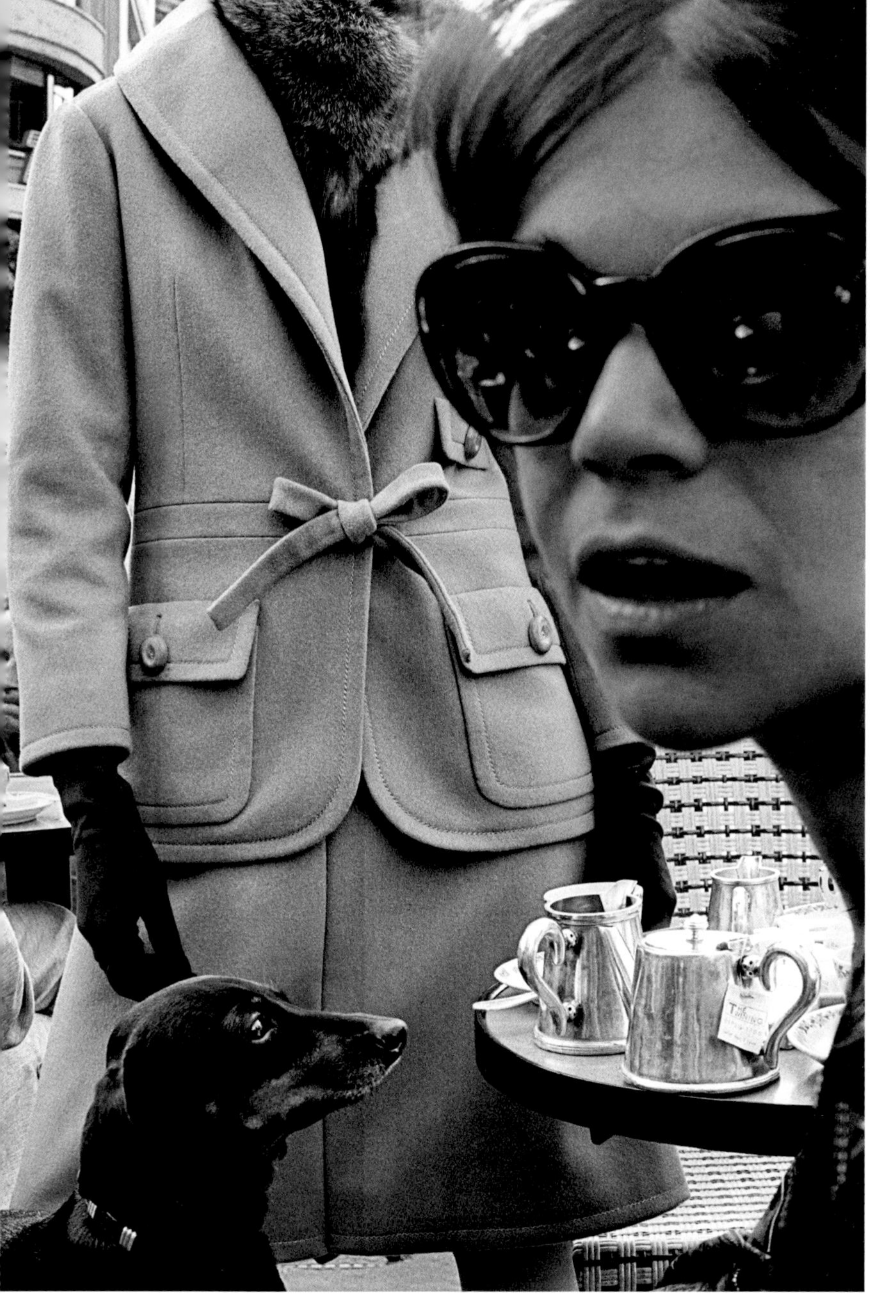

32. For *Harper's Bazaar*, New York, 1961.

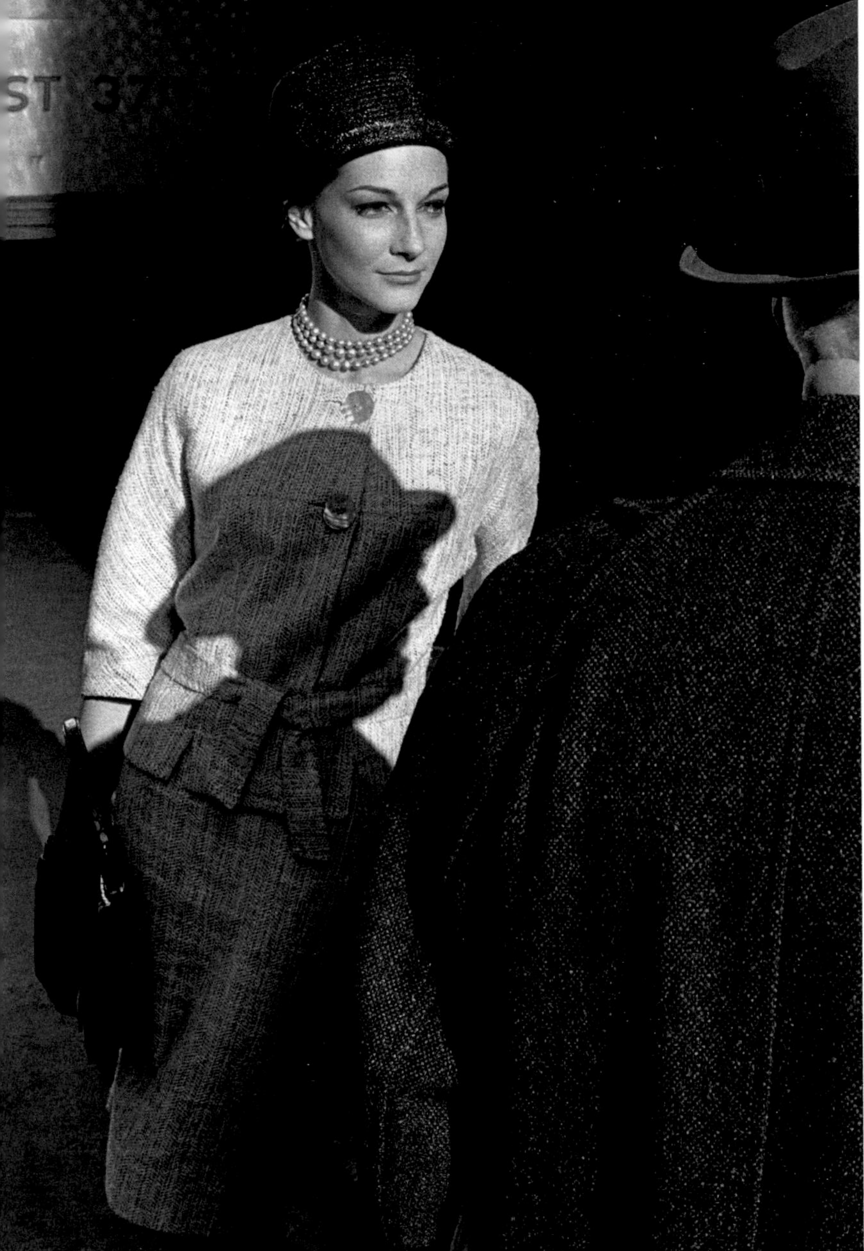

33. Deborah Dixon, for *Harper's Bazaar*, Rome, 1962.

Overleaf:
34. Deborah Dixon, for *Harper's Bazaar*, Rome, 1962.
35. Deborah Dixon and Federico Fellini, for *Harper's Bazaar*, Rome, 1962.

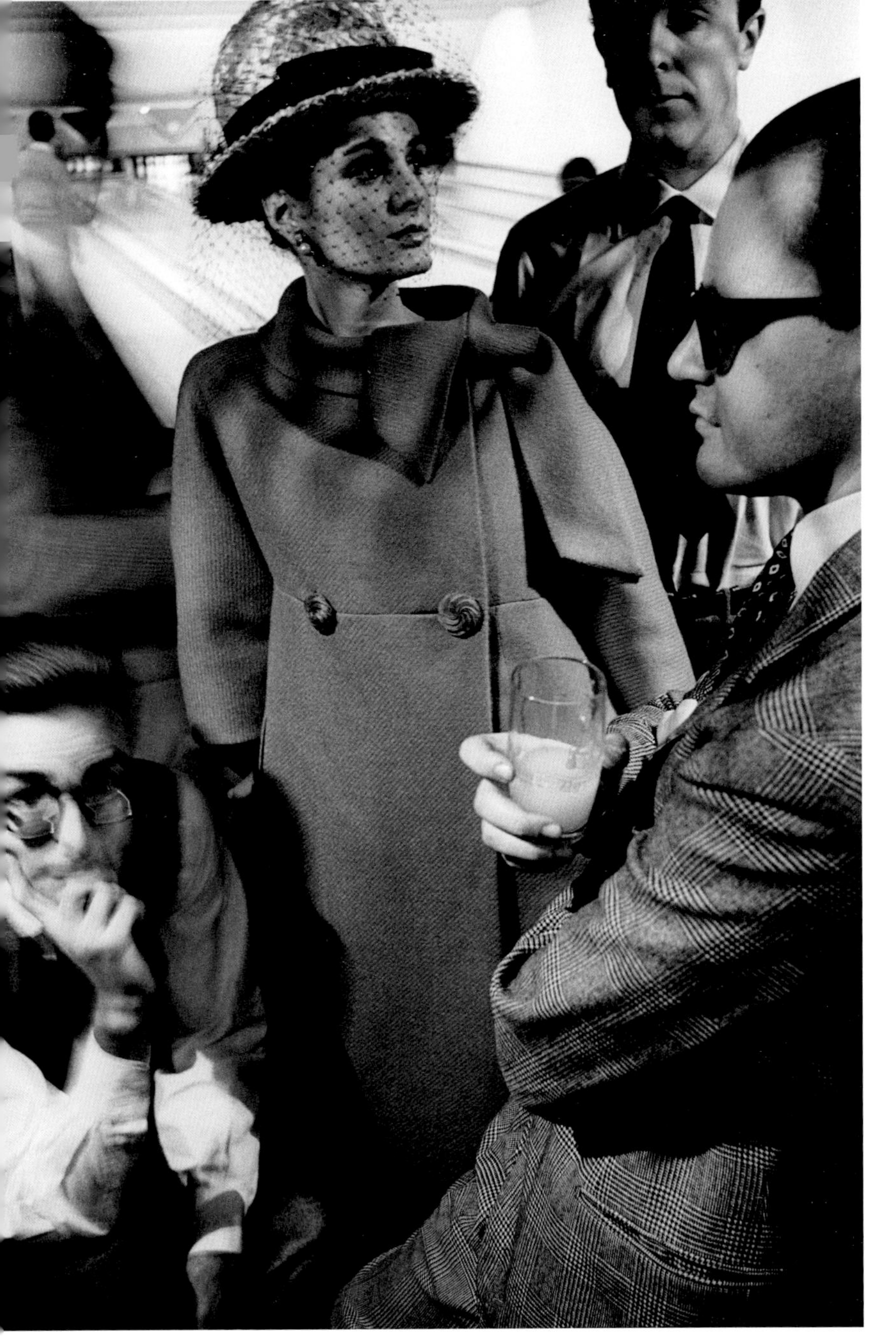

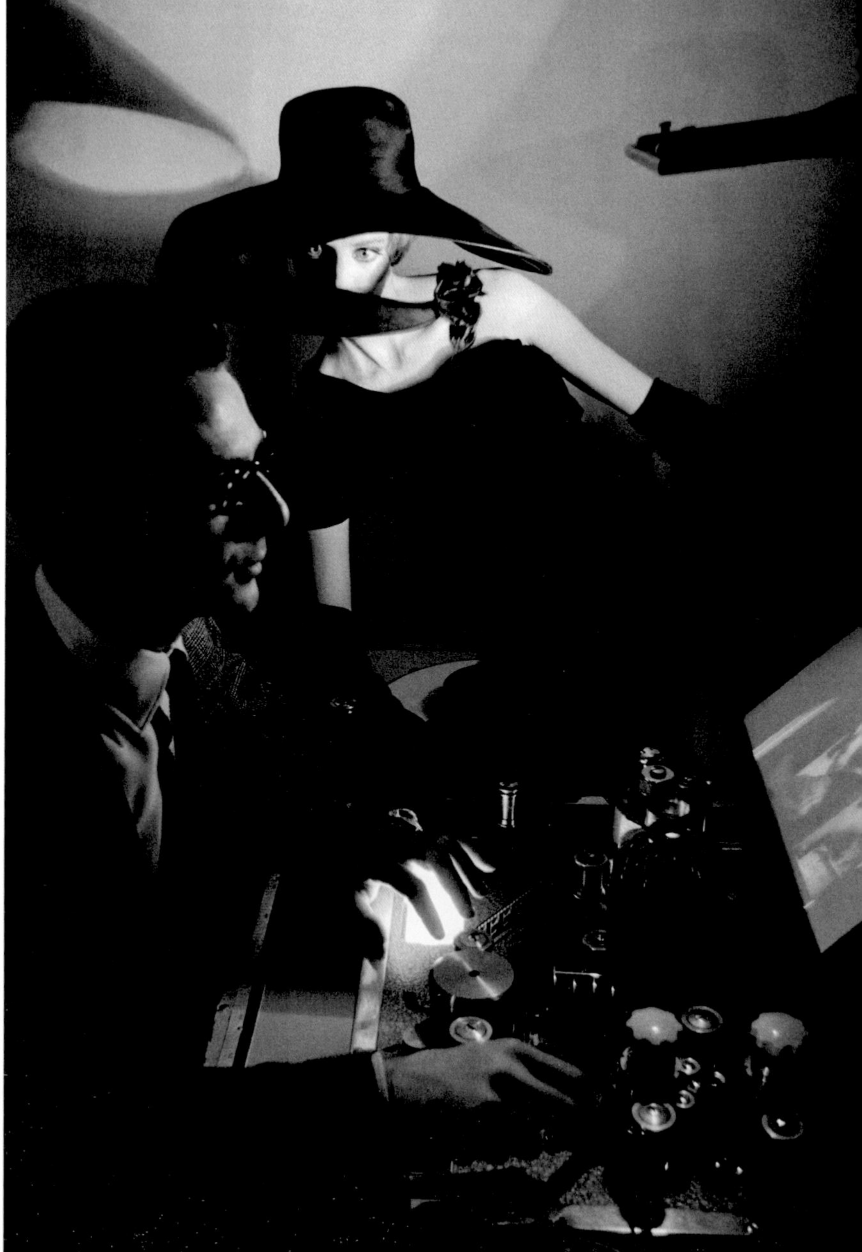

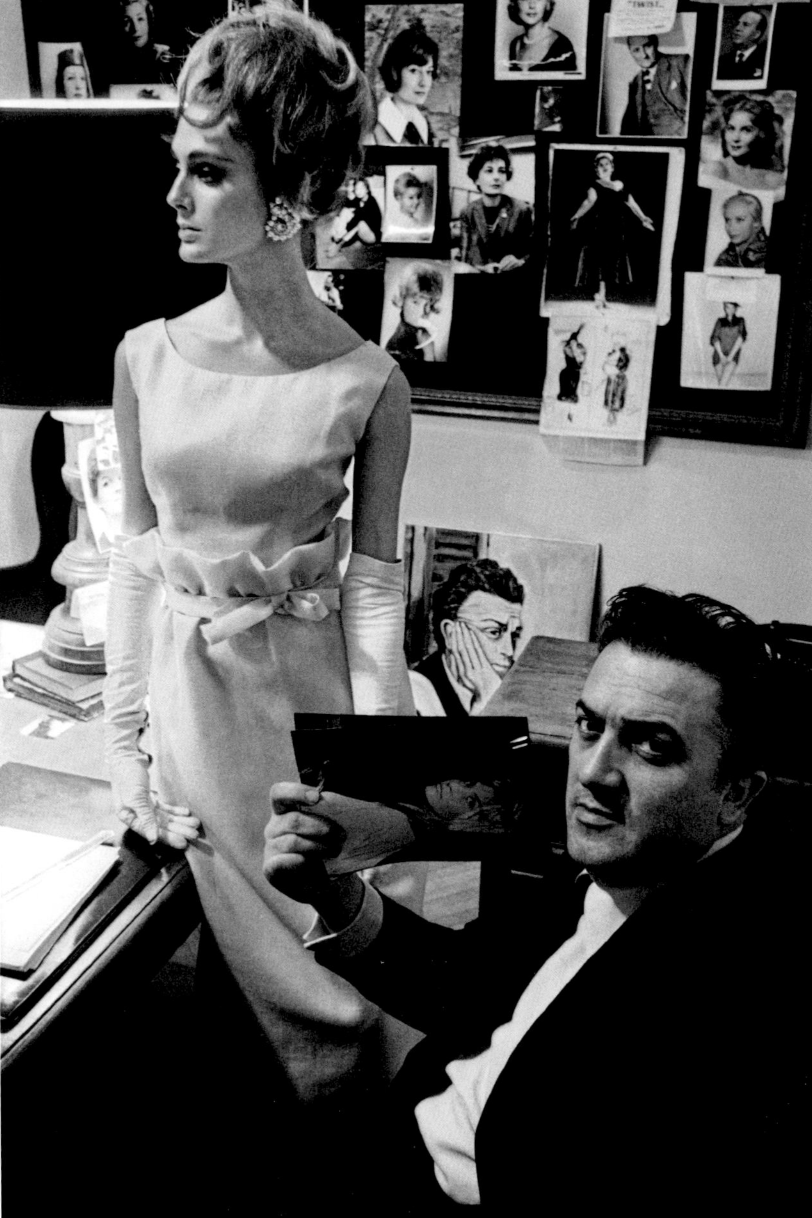

36. Deborah Dixon, Piazza di Spagna,
for *Harper's Bazaar*, Rome, 1962.

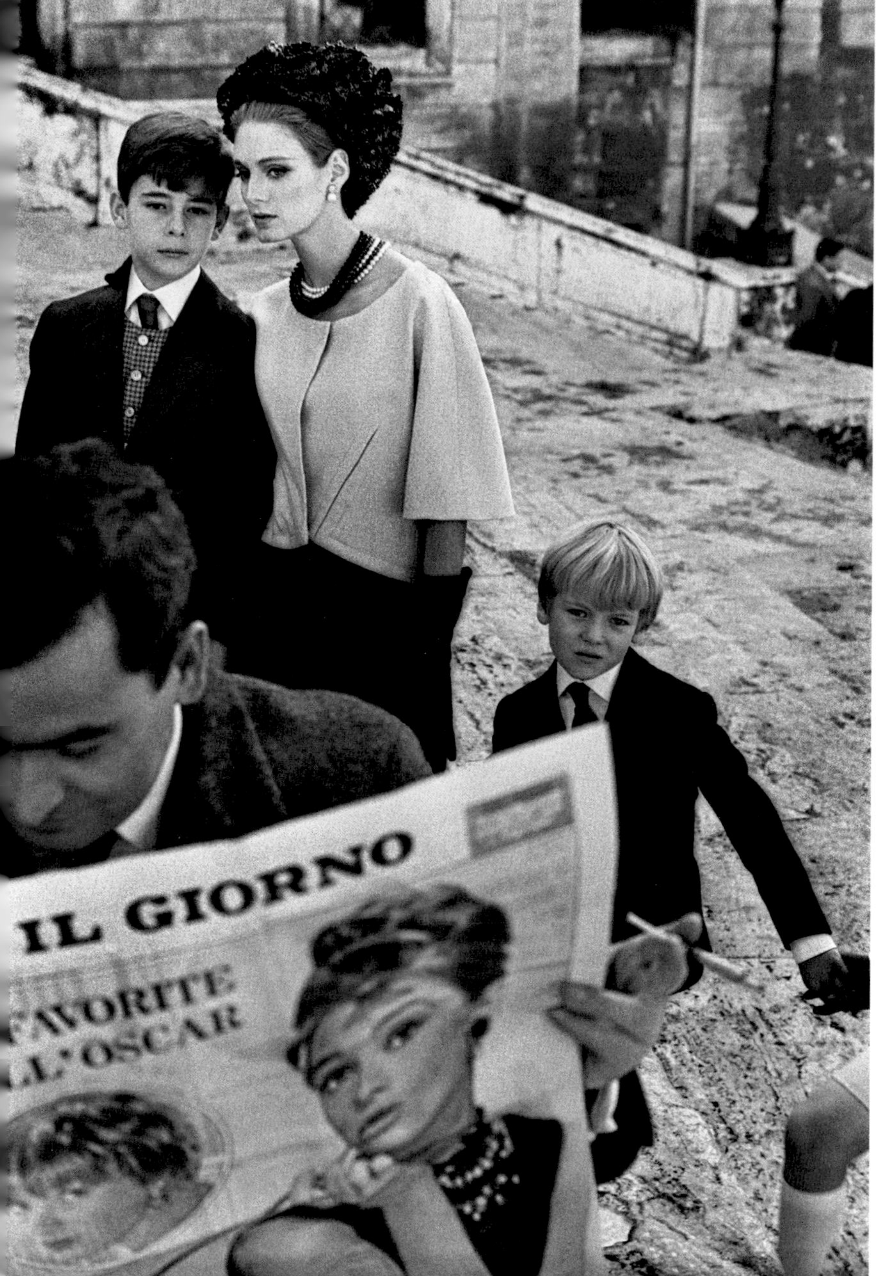
IL GIORNO
FAVORITE
ALL'OSCAR

37. Judy Dent, for *Élégance*, Paris, 1961.

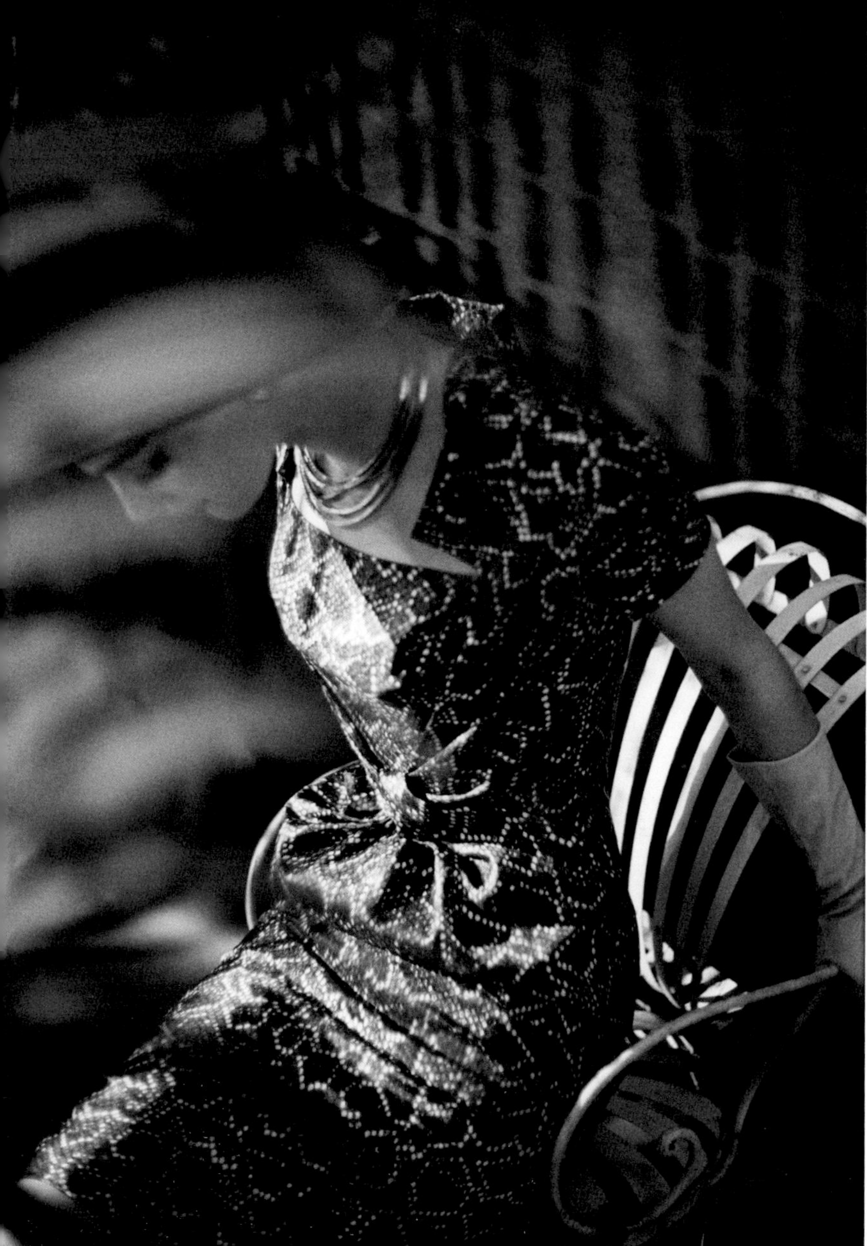

38. Iris Bianchi and Agnès Varda,
for *Harper's Bazaar*, Paris, 1962.

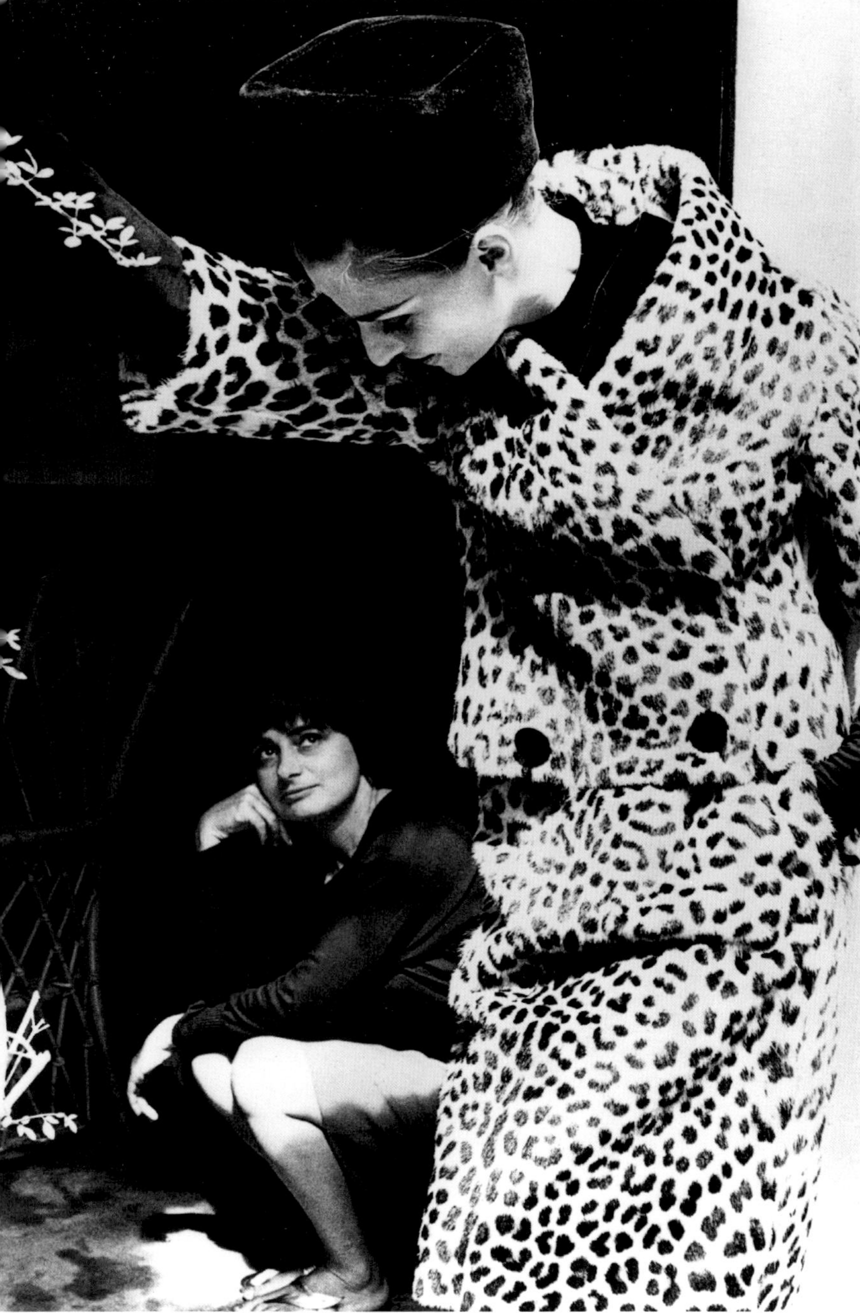

39. Judy Dent, for *Vogue* UK, Yorkshire, 1961.

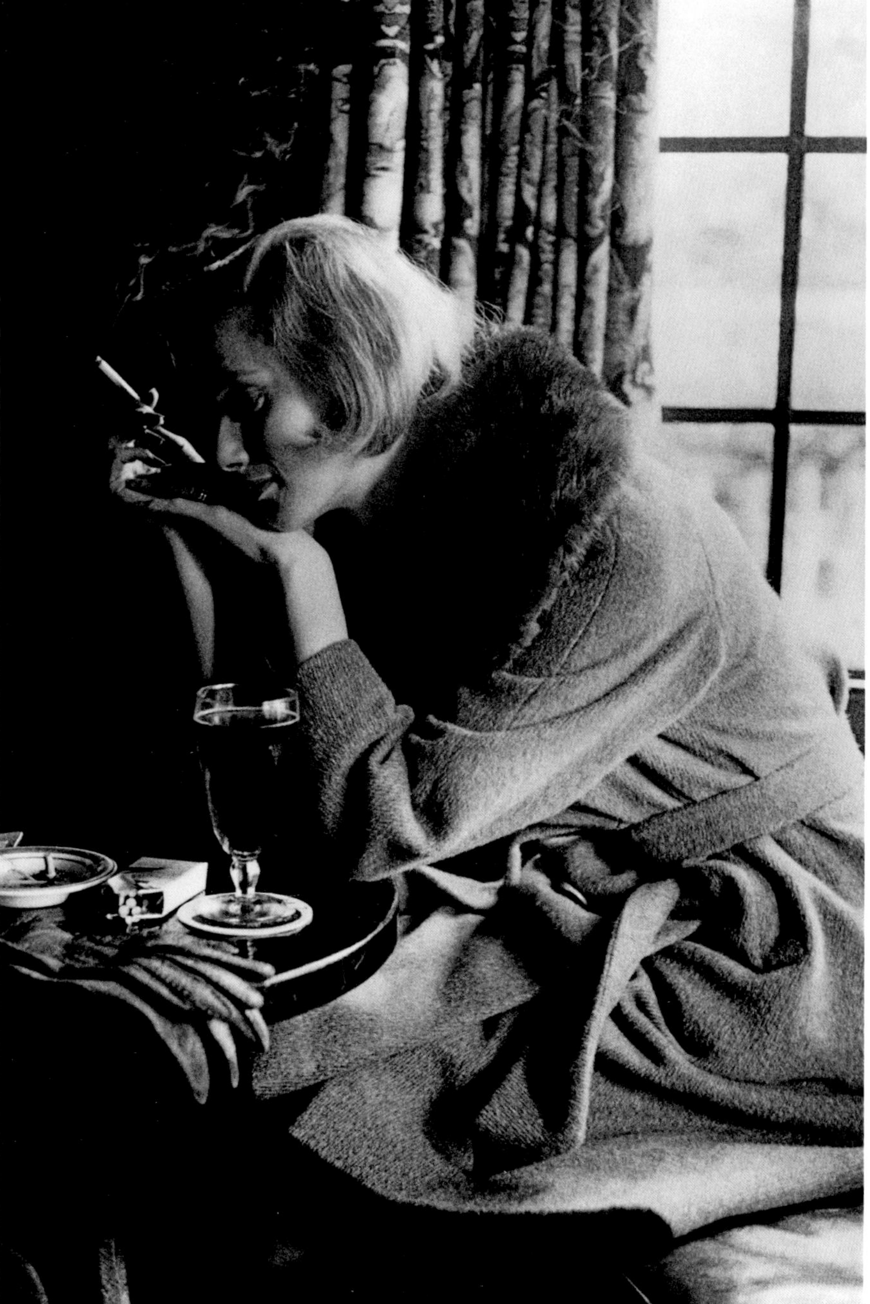

40. Ros Watkins, for *Vogue* UK, Yorkshire, 1961.

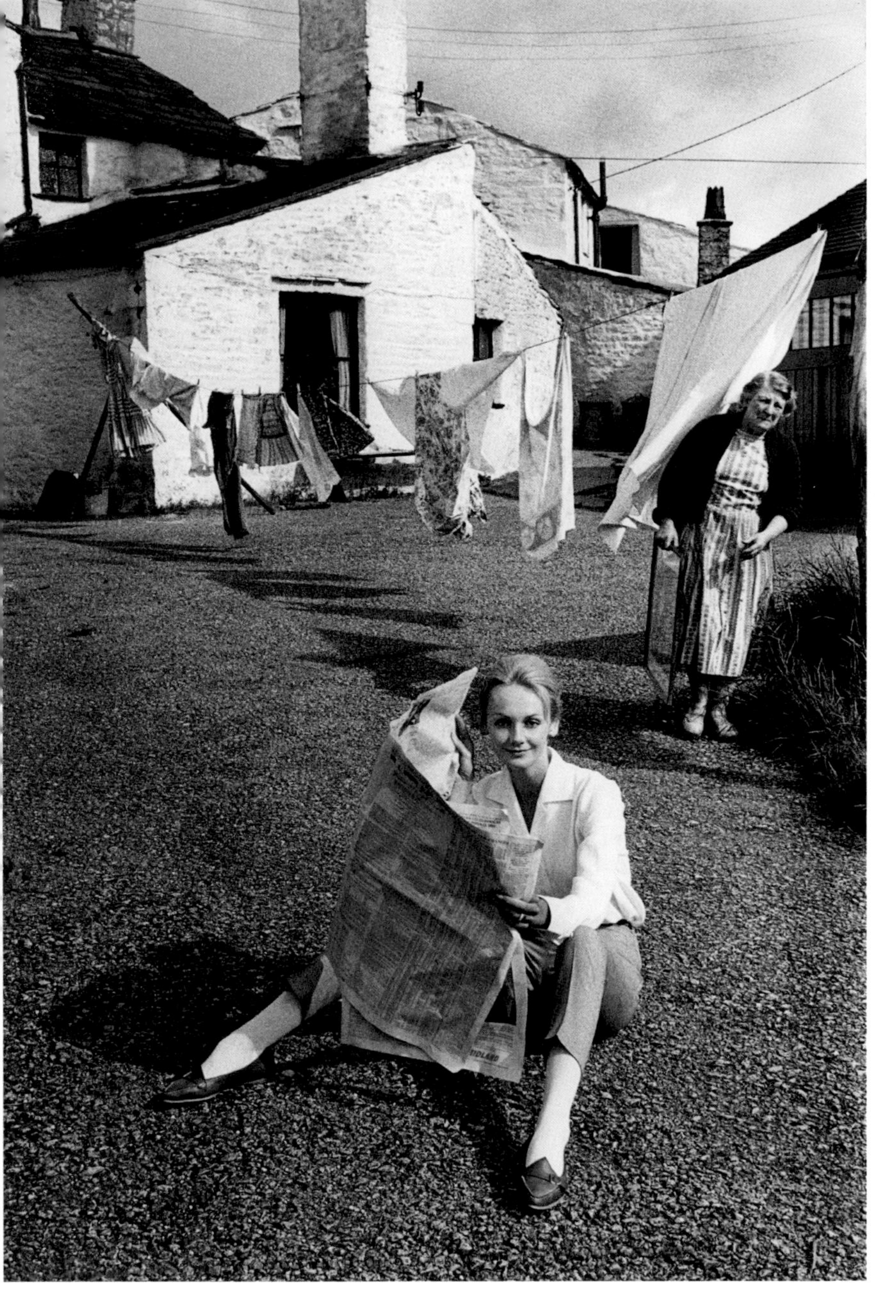

41. Judy Dent, rue du Parc-Montsouris, Paris, 1961.

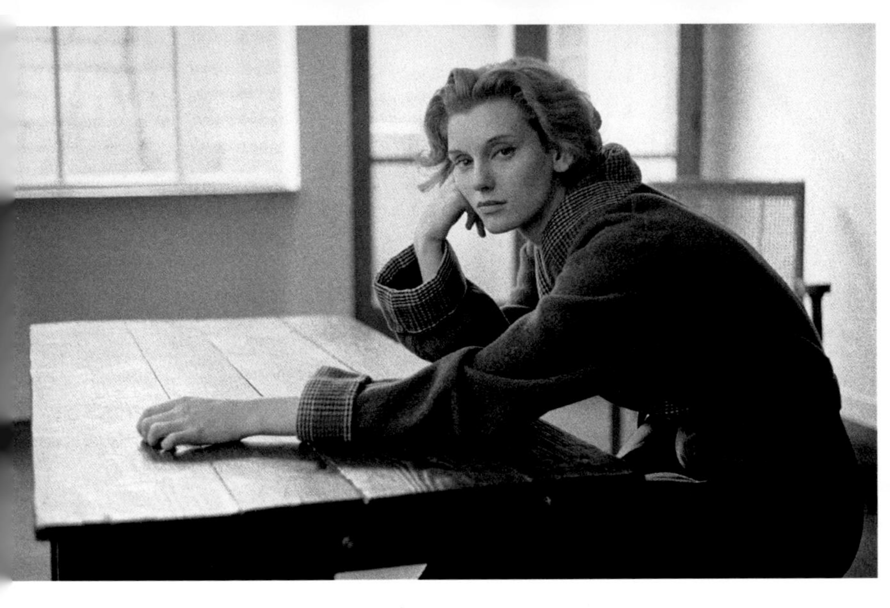

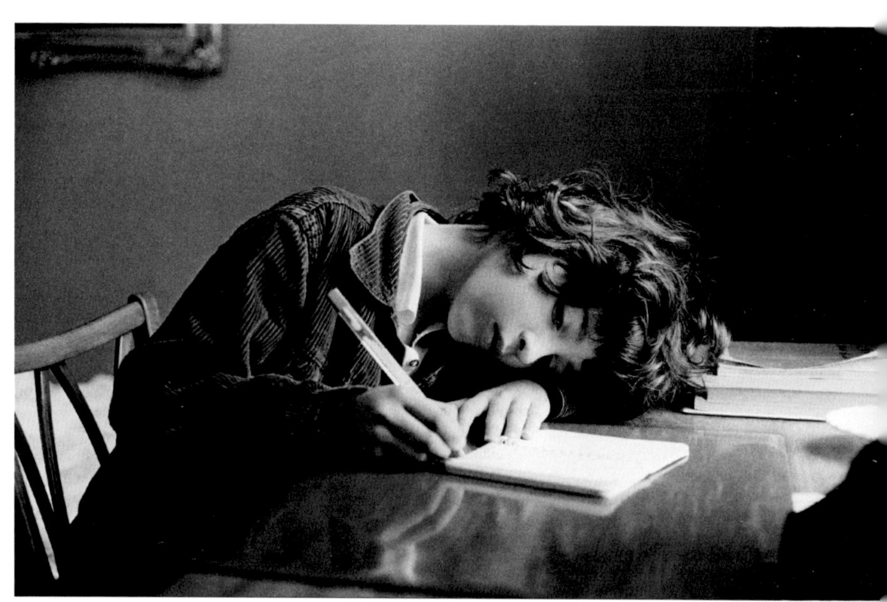

42. Marco, Sweden, 1969.

43. Lorenzo and Mate, rue Bocquillon, Paris, 1964.

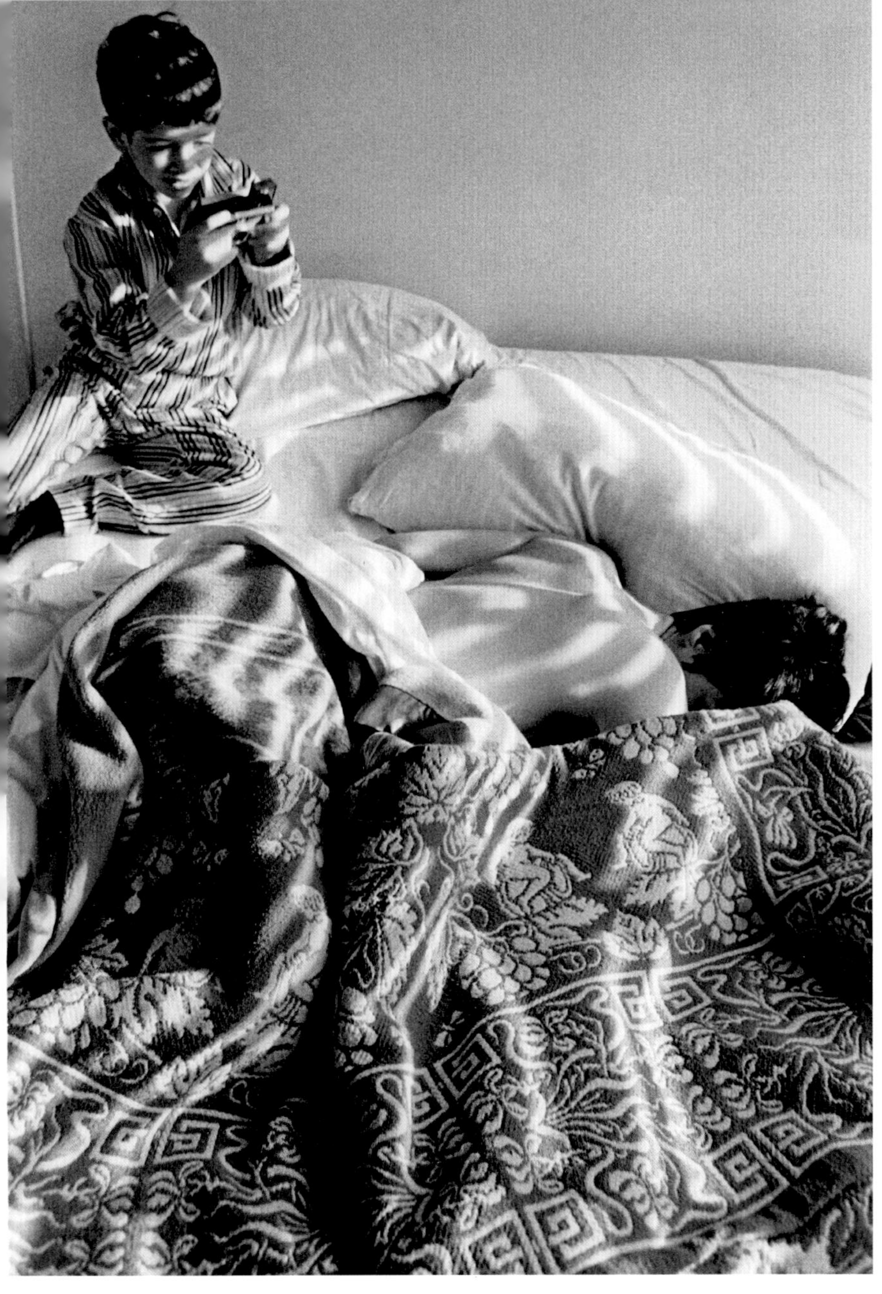

44. Mate and Lorenzo, Paris, 1957.

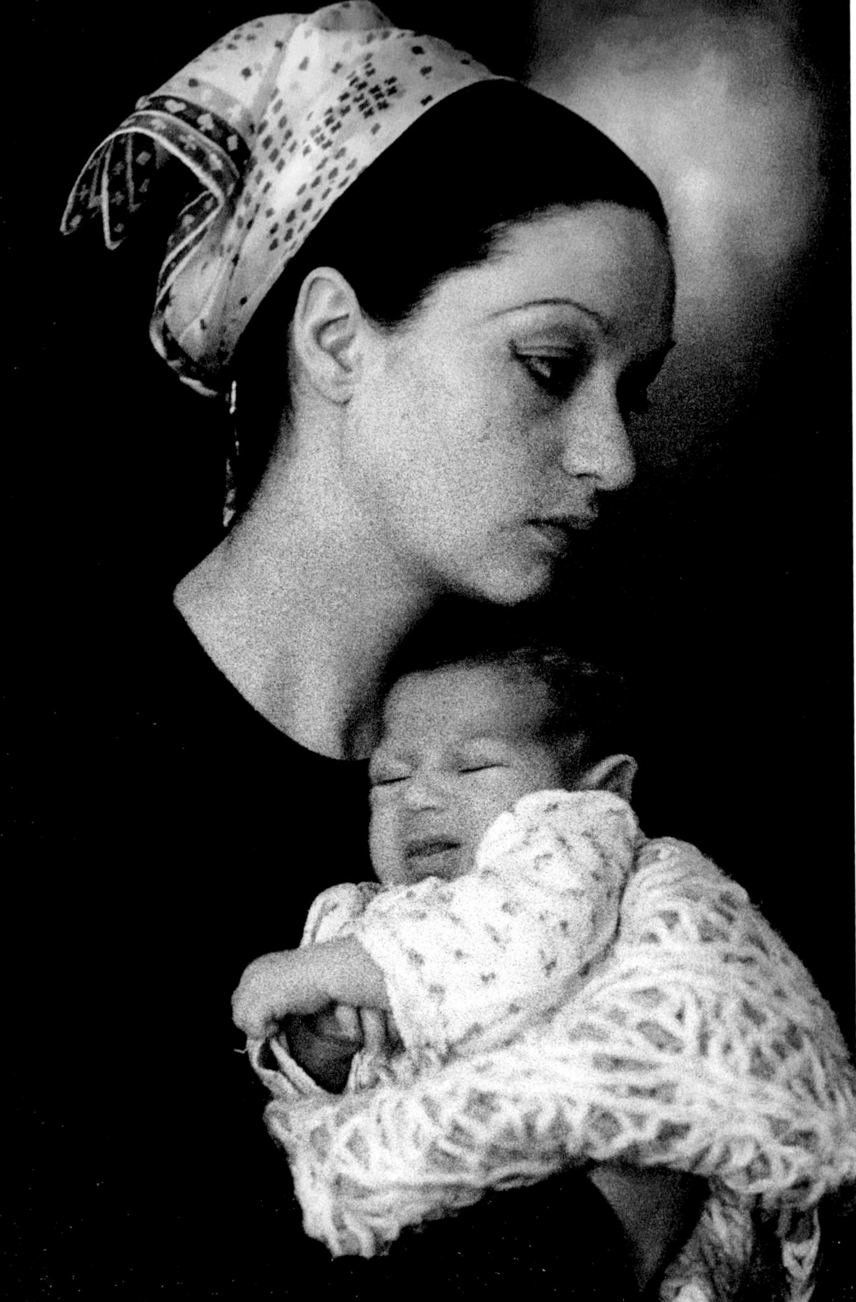

45. Mate, rue Bocquillon, Paris, 1964.

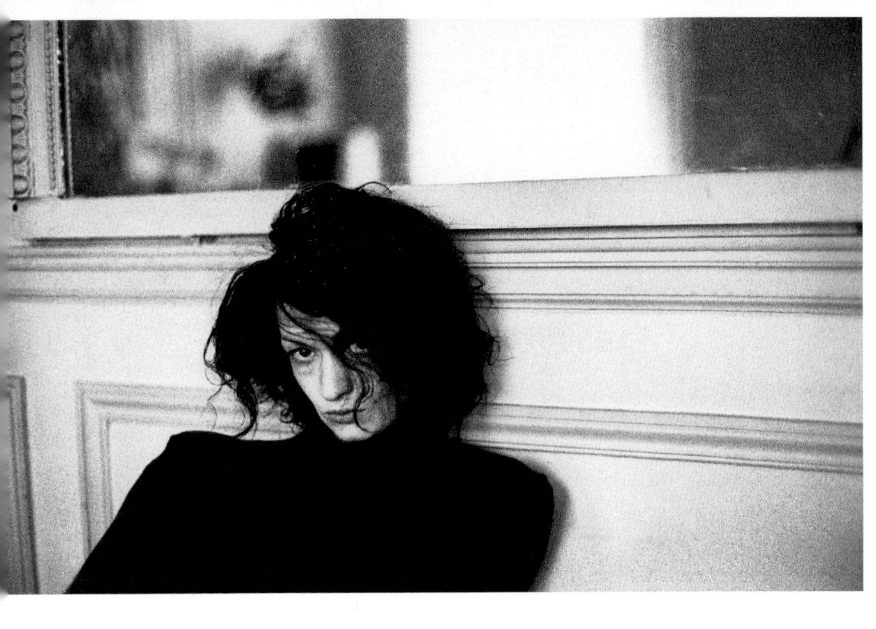

46. Tel Aviv, 1962.

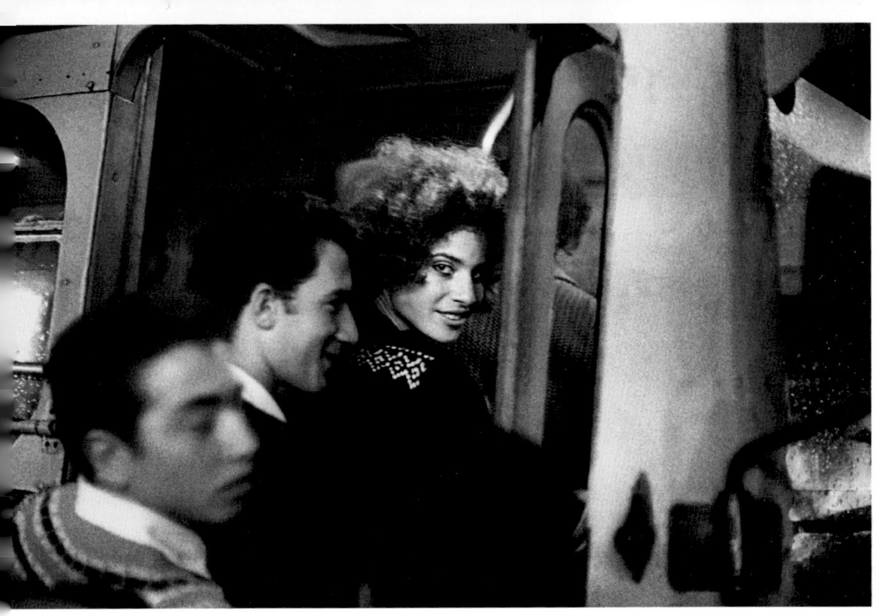

47. Teenagers, Tokyo, 1963.

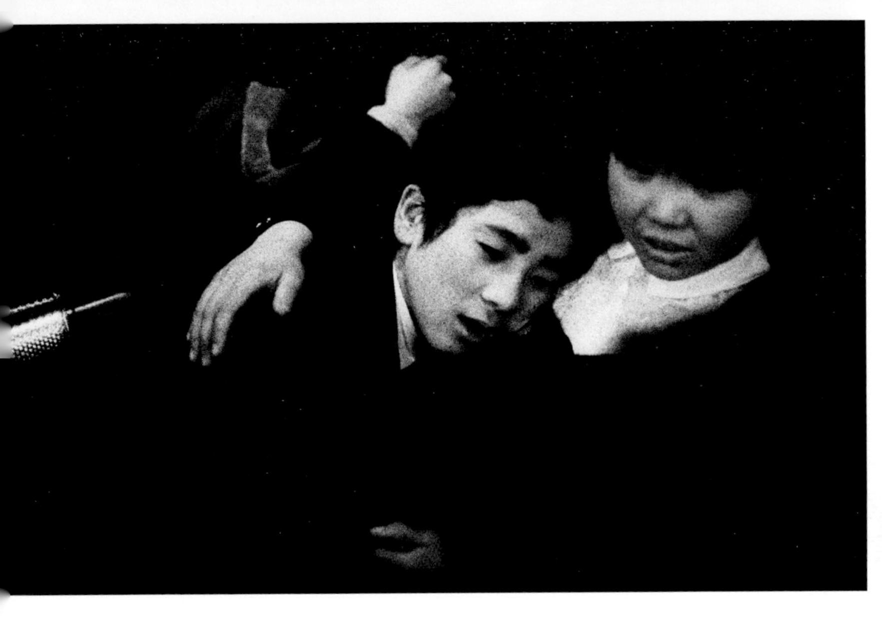

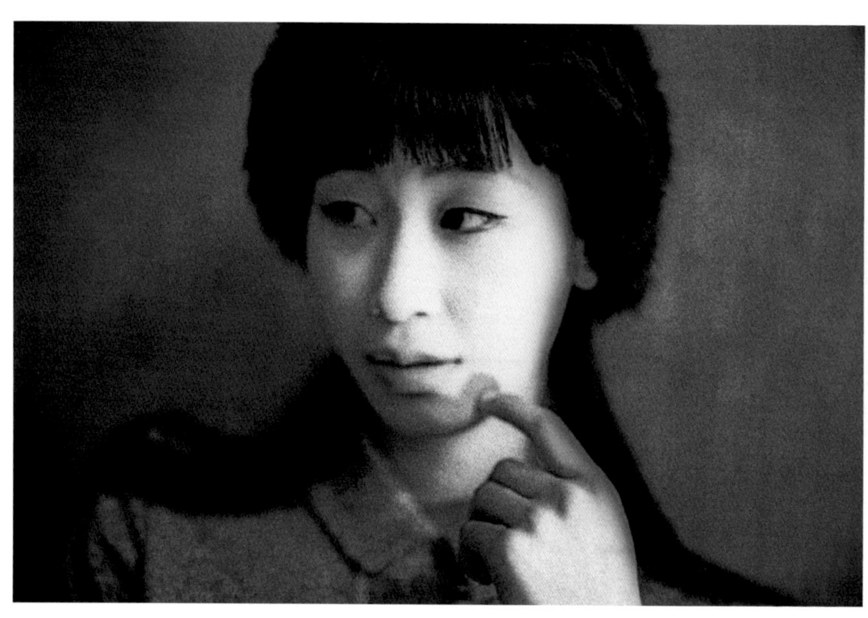

48–49. Hostesses, Tokyo, 1963.

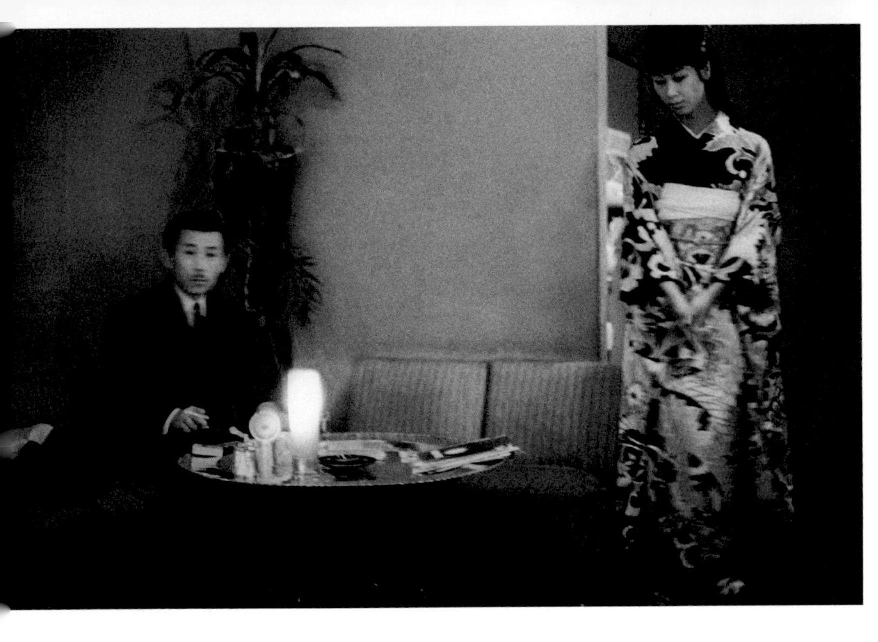

50. Christmas Eve in a bar for sailors, Calcutta, 1962.

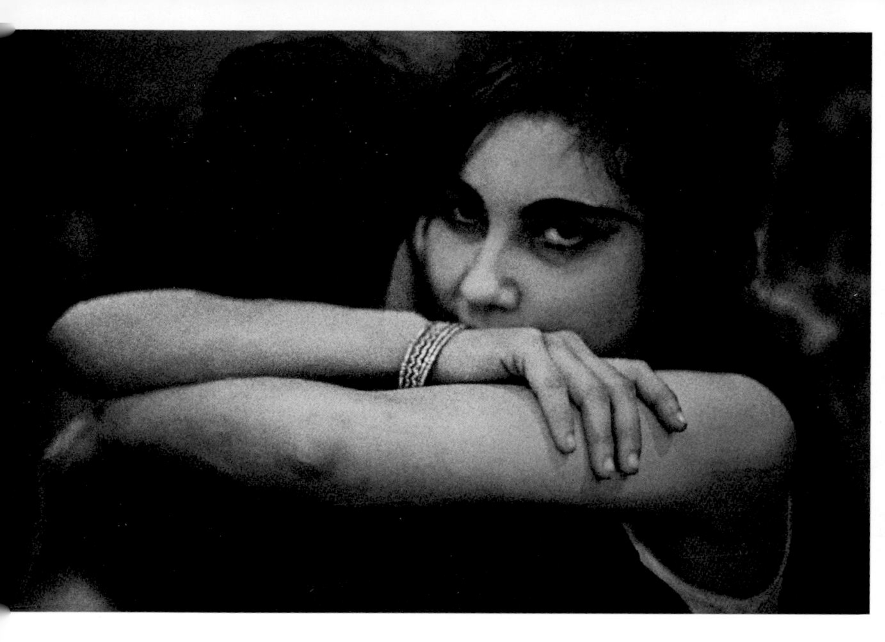

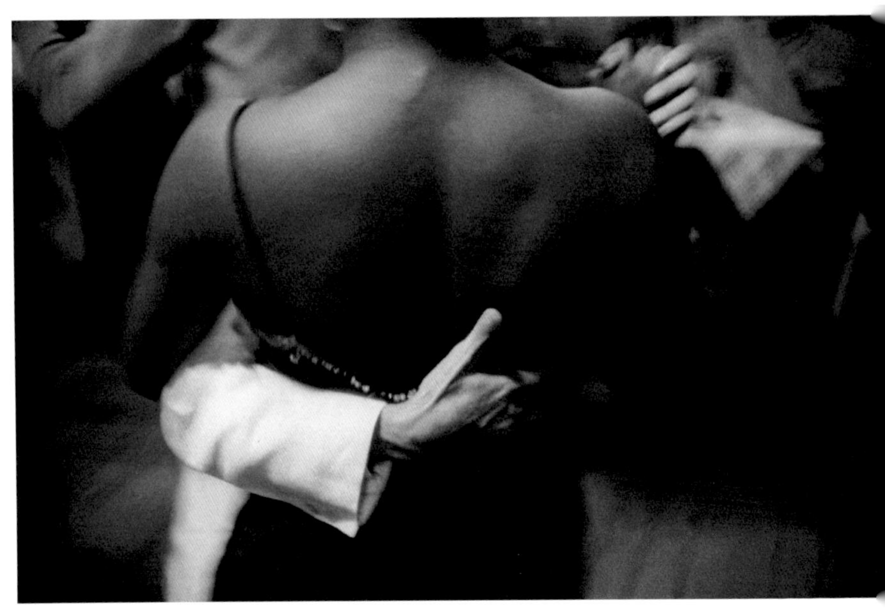

51. Rio de Janeiro, 1963.

52. Christmas Eve in a bar for sailors, Calcutta, 1962.

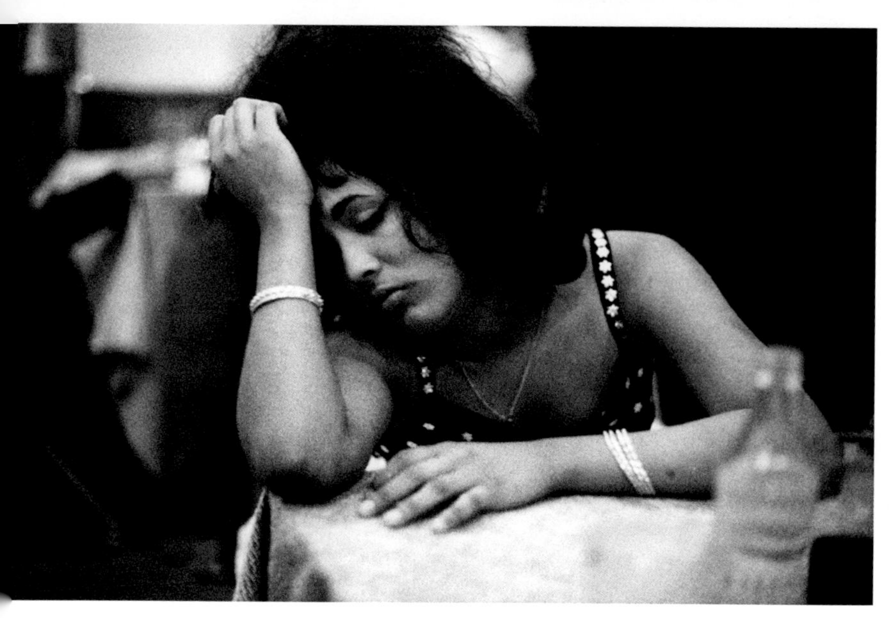

53. Macumba, Rio de Janeiro, 1963.

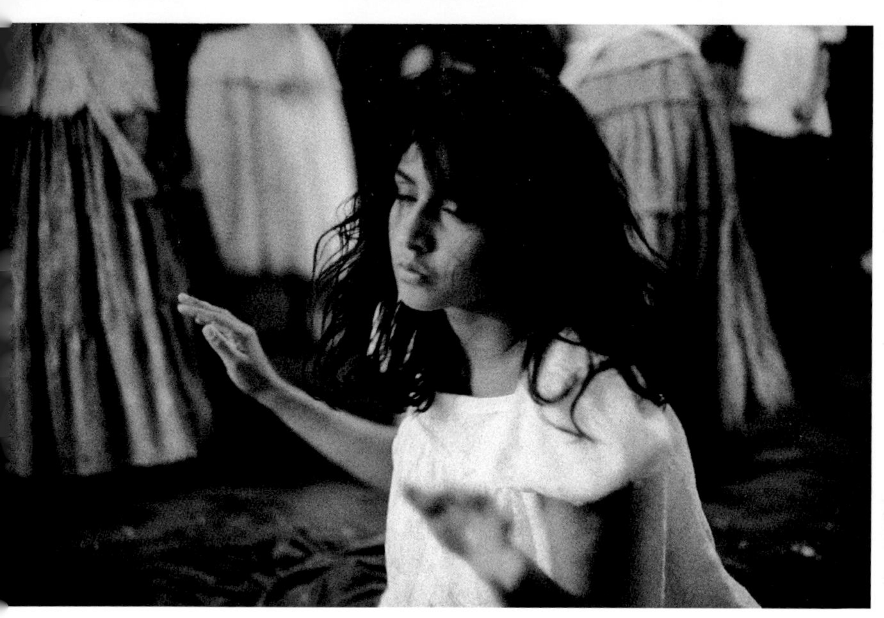

54. Caracas, 1963.

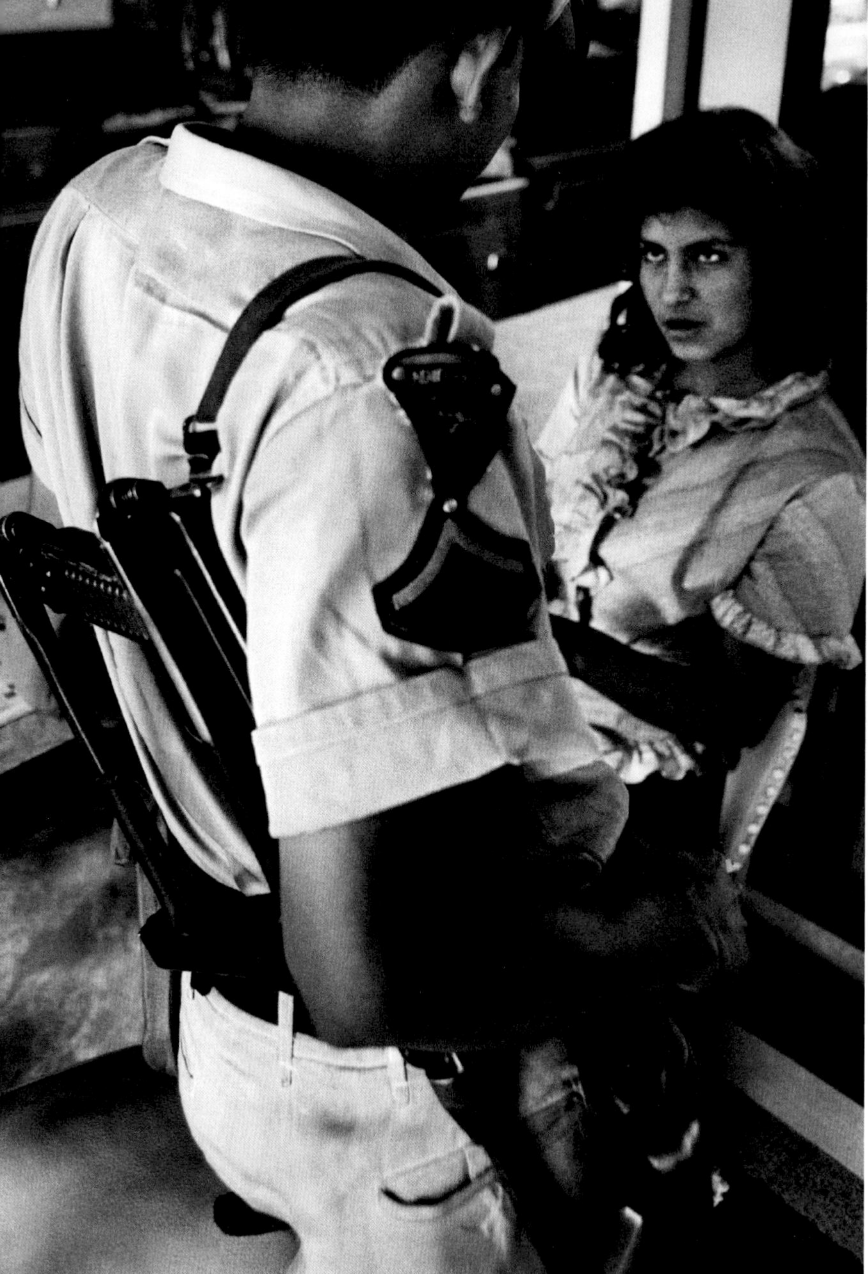

55. Sydney, 1963.

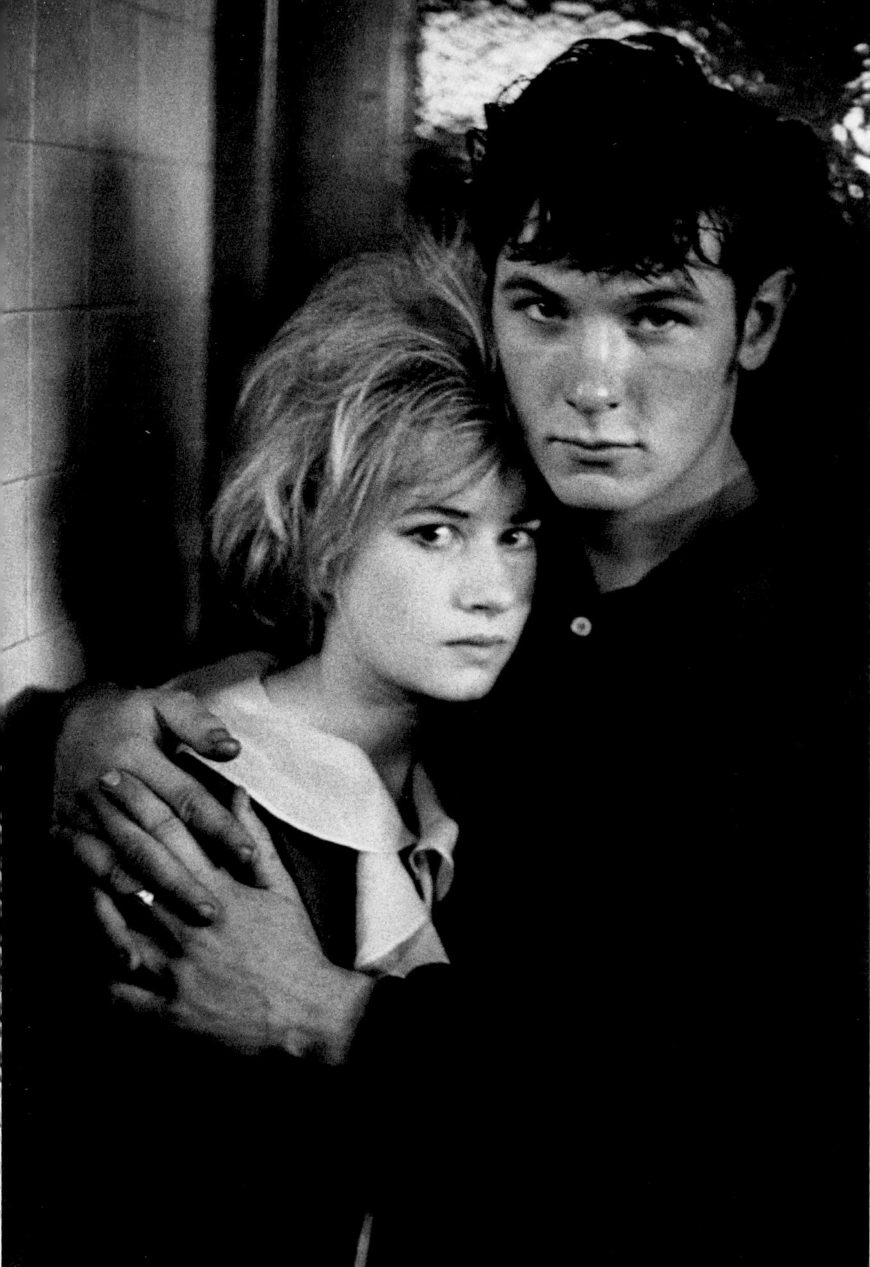

56. Politicians, Caracas, 1963.

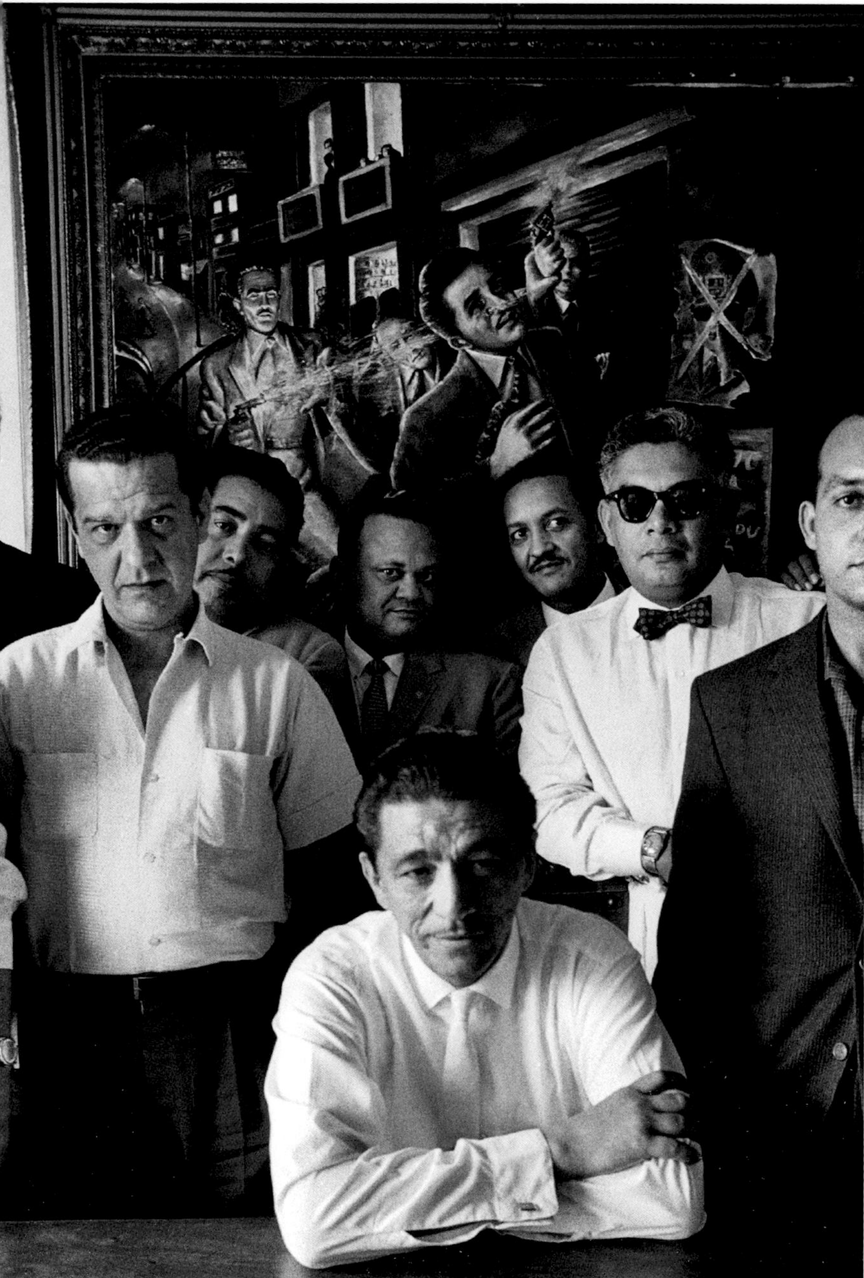

57. Television studio, Cairo, 1962.

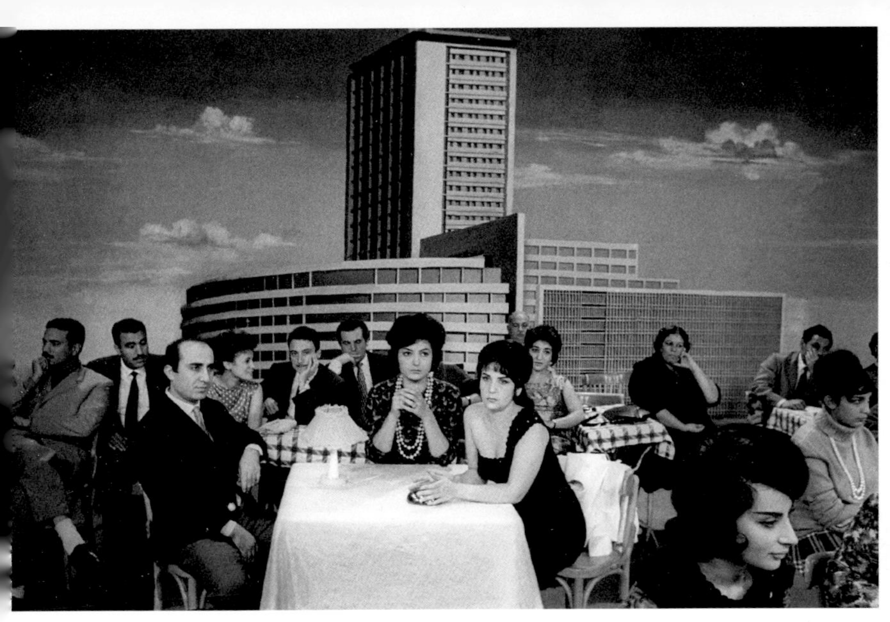

58. Margrit Ramme, for *Queen*, Paris, 1970.

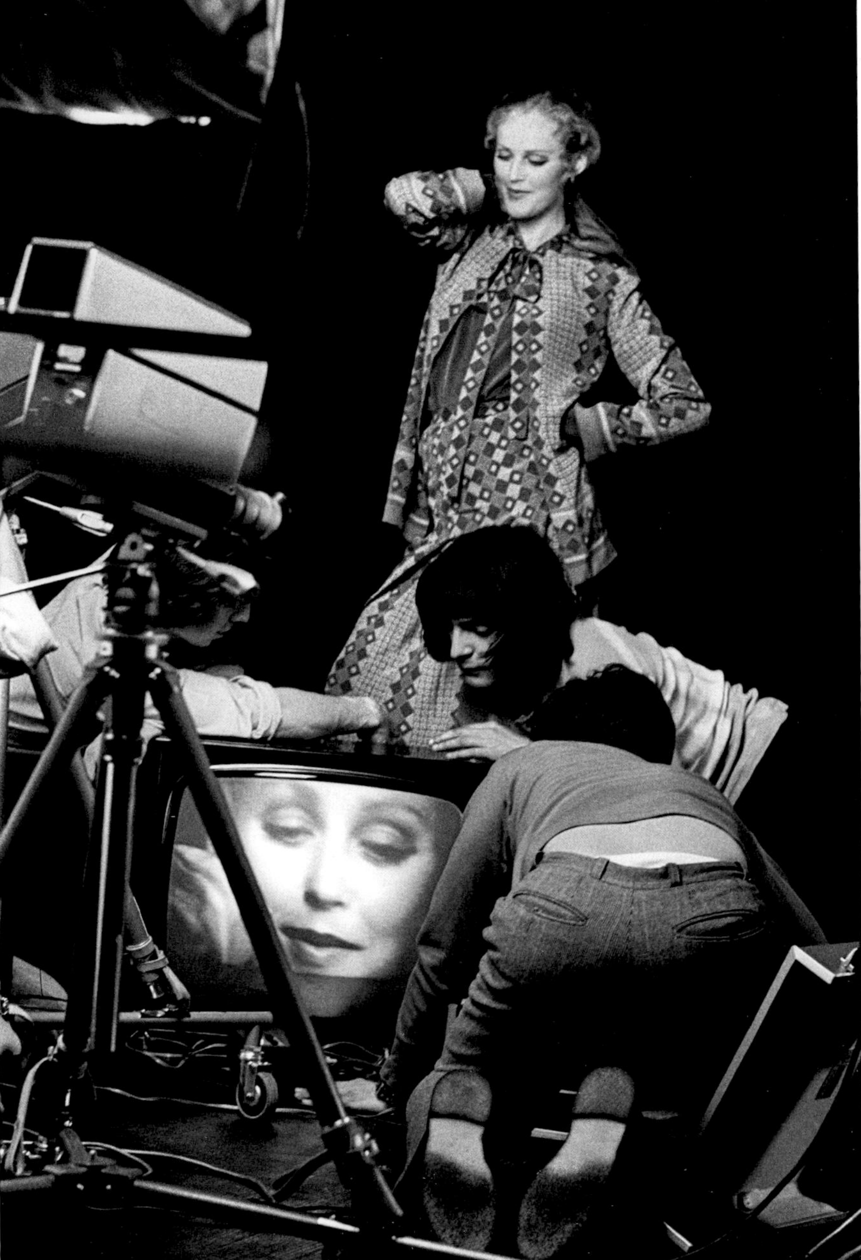

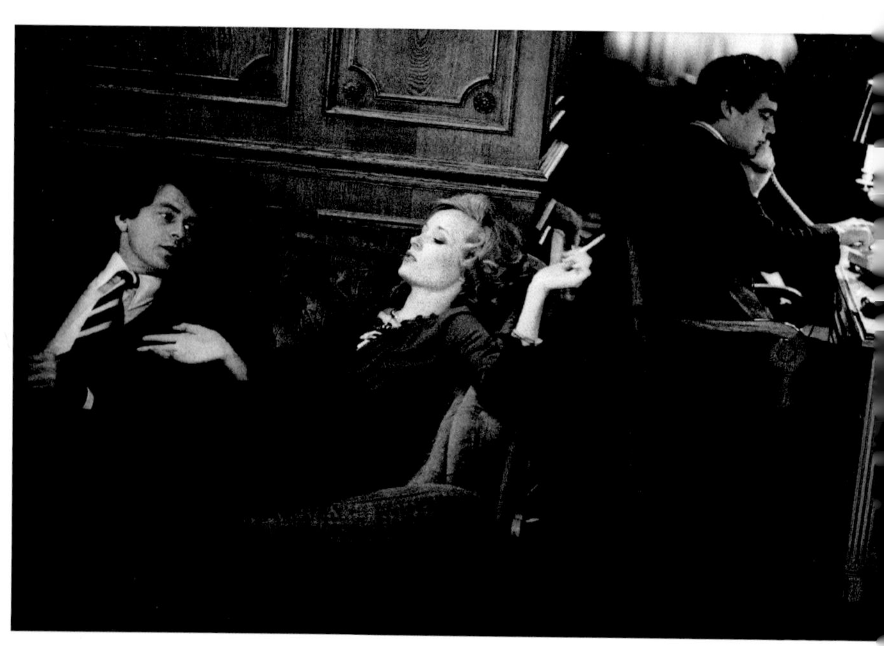

59. For *Vogue* France, Paris, 1976.

60. Margrit Ramme, for *Queen*, Paris, 1970.

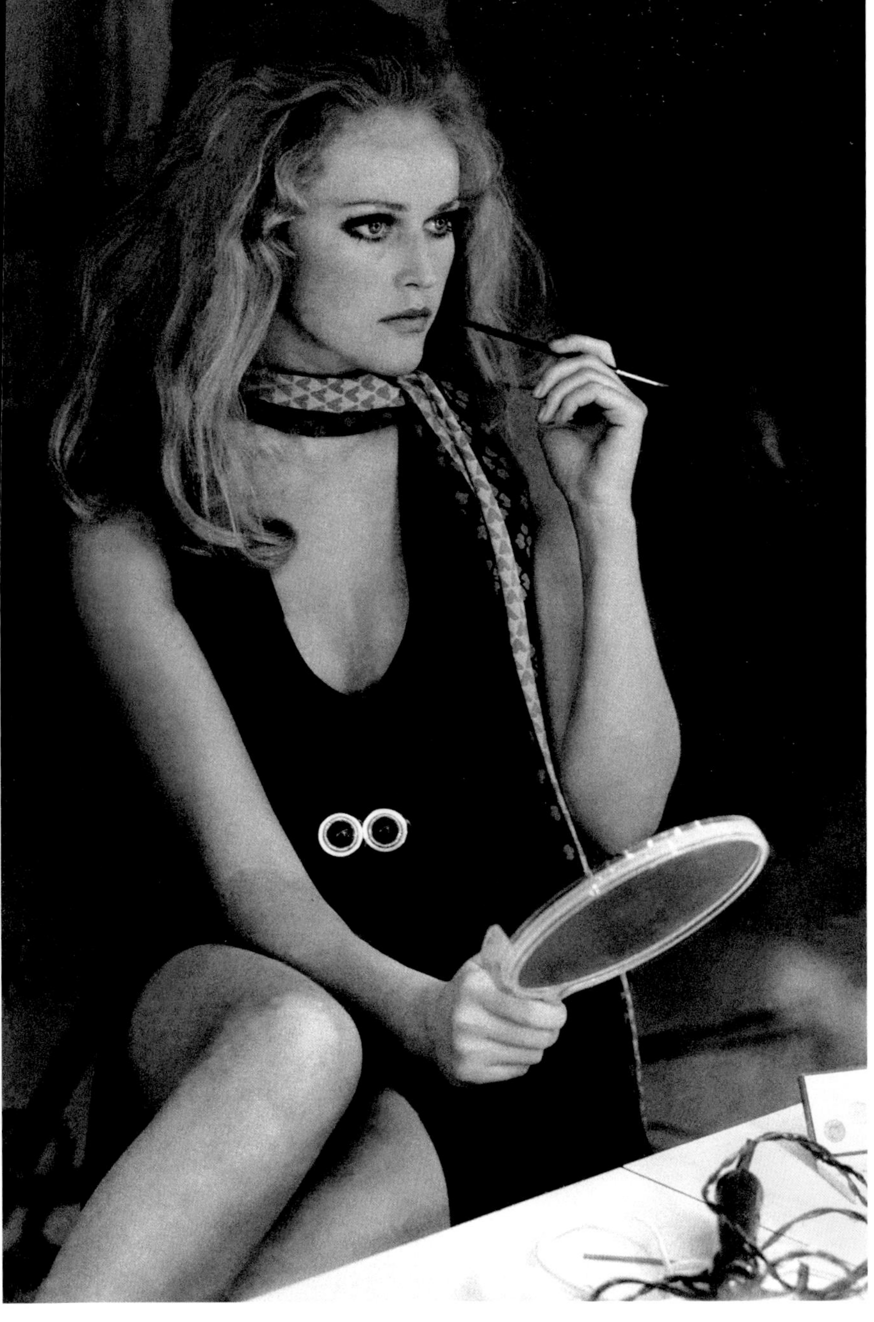

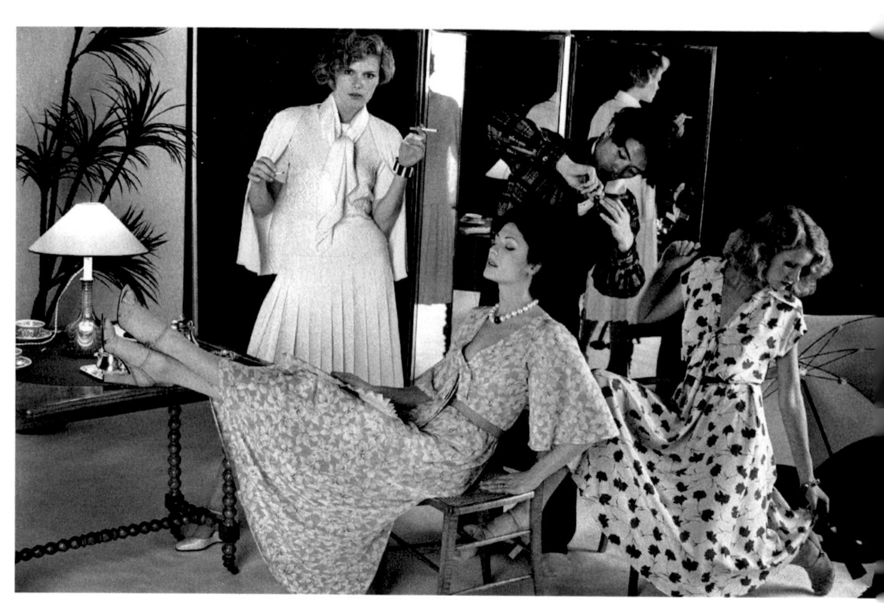

61. For *Vogue* France, Paris, 1974.
62. Chris O'Connor, for *Vogue* France, Paris, 1974.

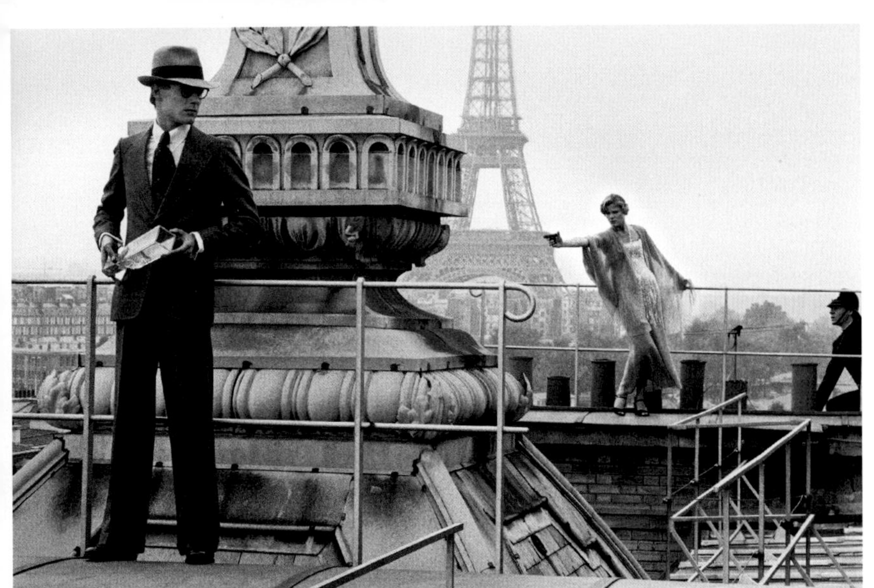

63. For *Stern*, Paris, 1974.

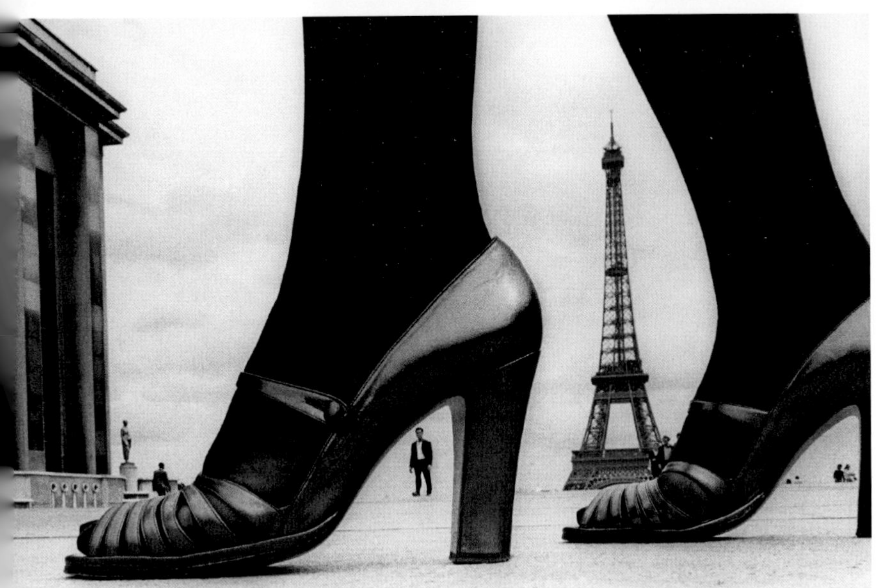

64. Alessandra Ferlini, for *Vogue* Italy, Paris, 1986.

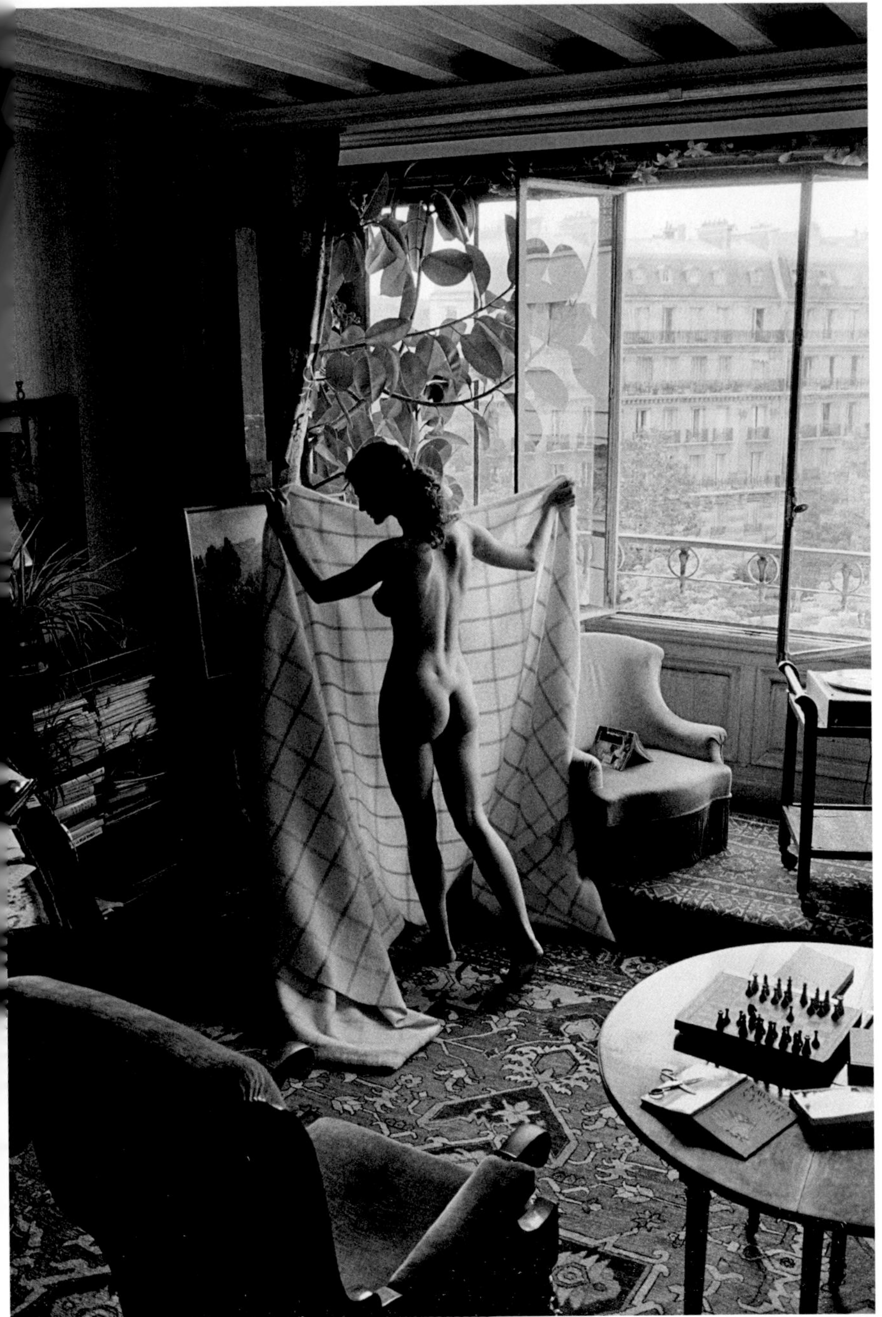

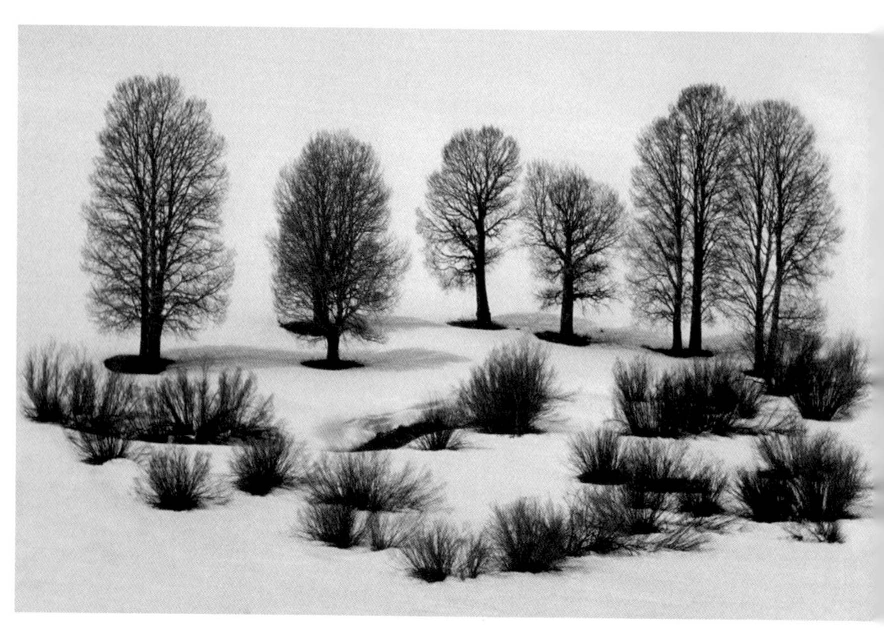

65. Poplars, Nevada, 1978.
66. Apple tree, Zurich, 1976.

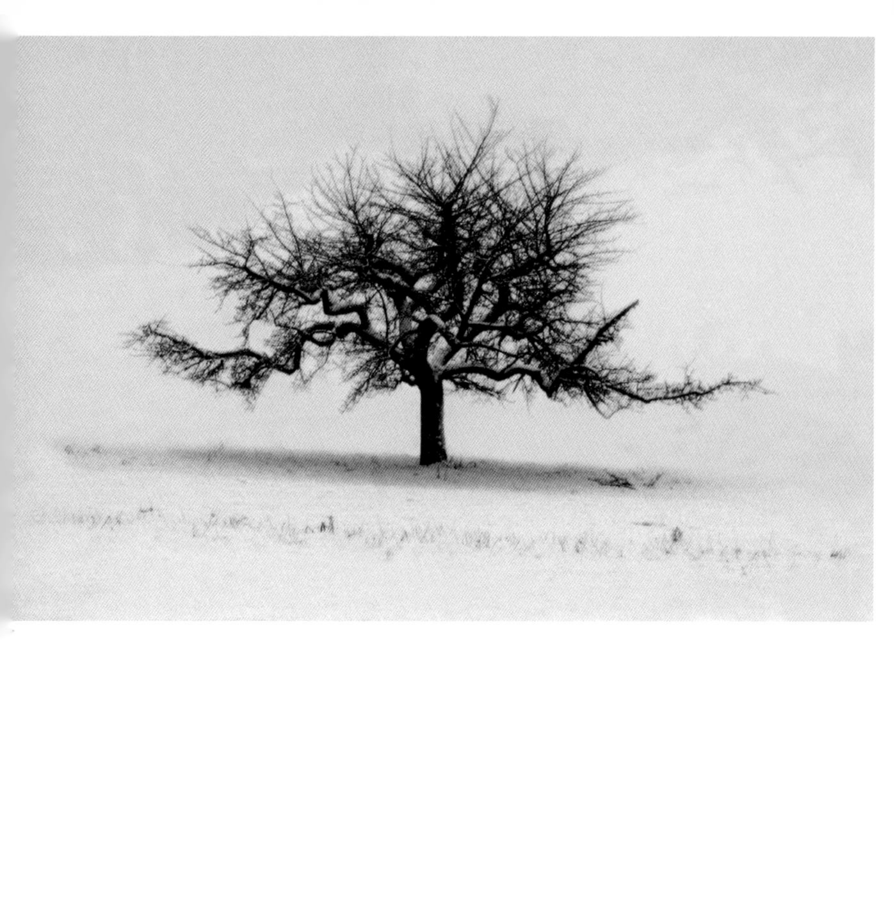

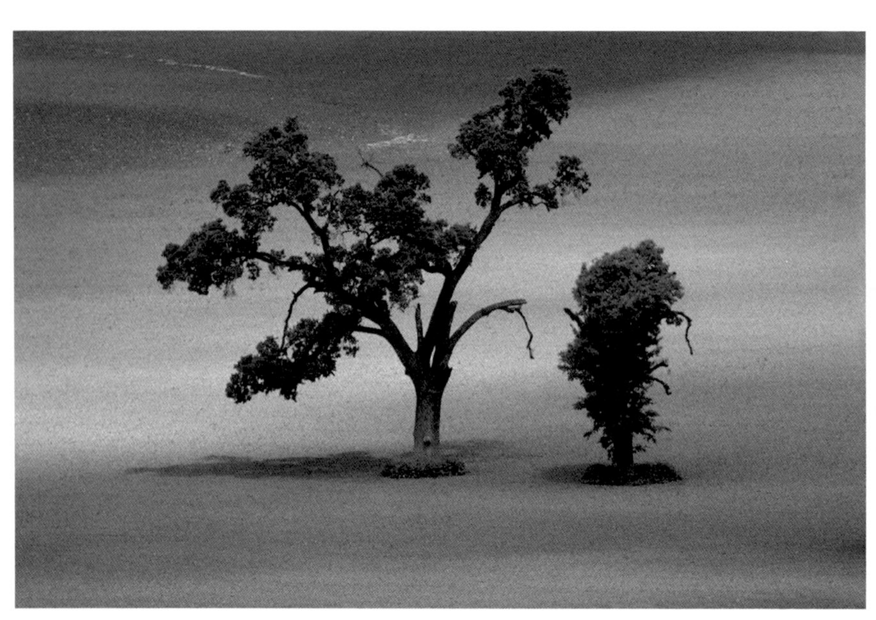

67. Oak trees, California, 1978.
68. Pine trees, Corsica, 1976.

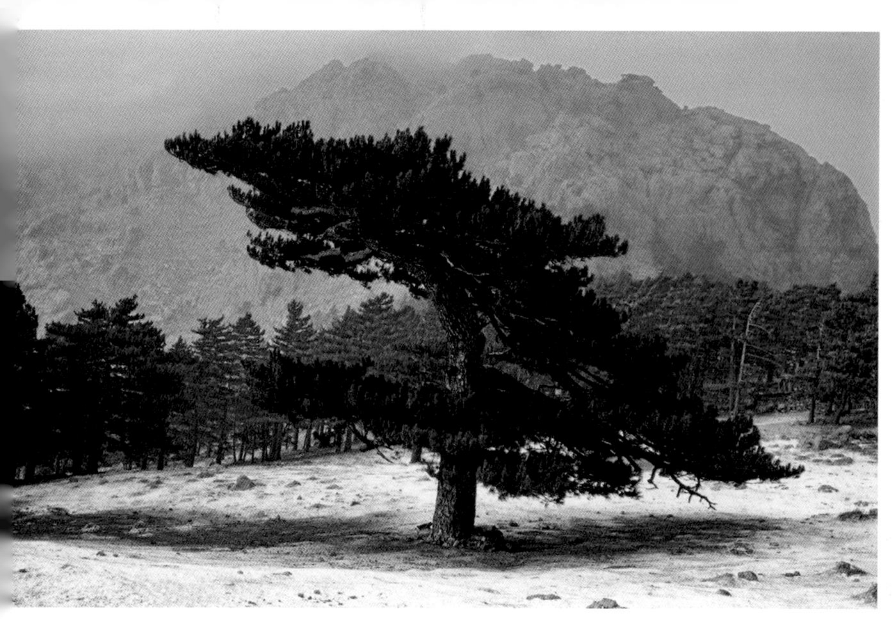

69. New York, 1983.

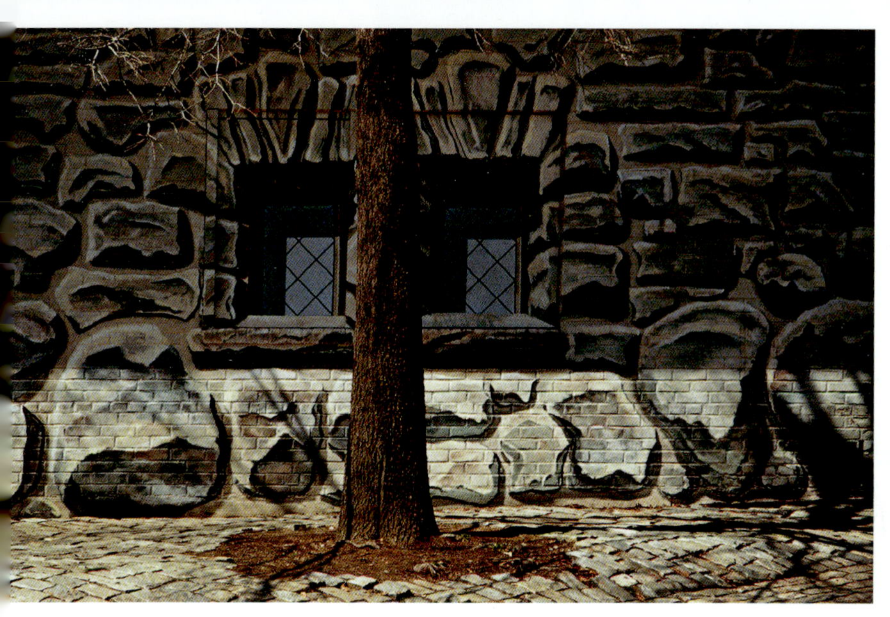

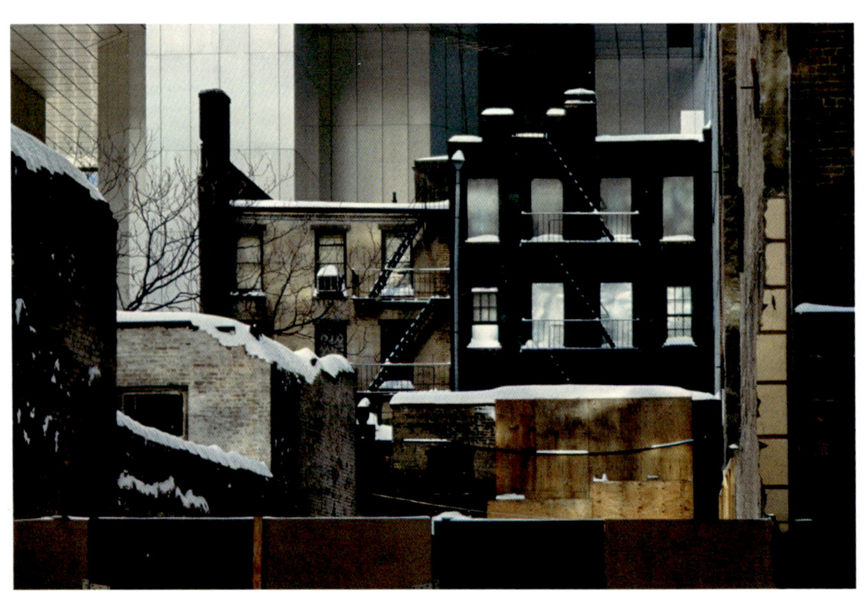

70. New York, 1983.
71. New York, 1984.

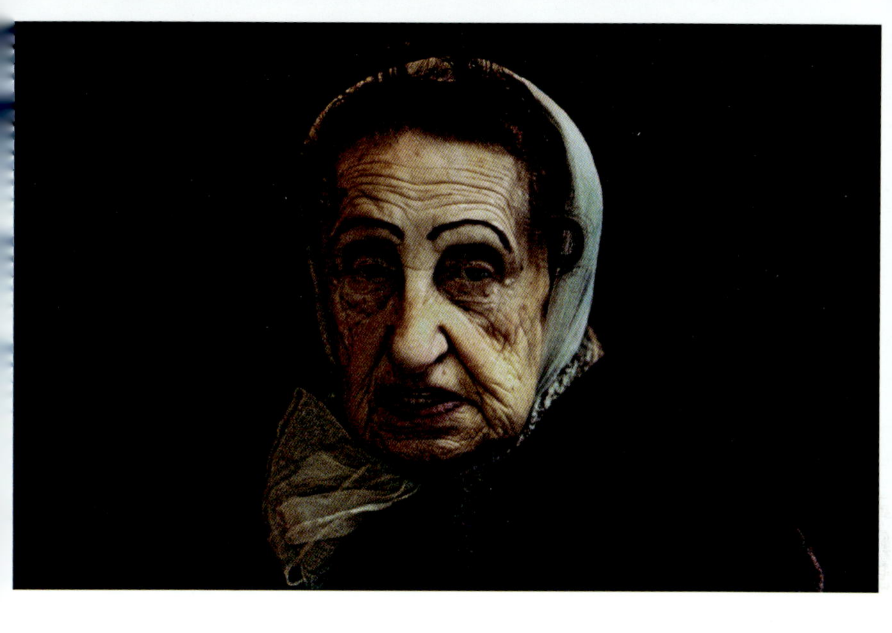

72. New York, 1984.

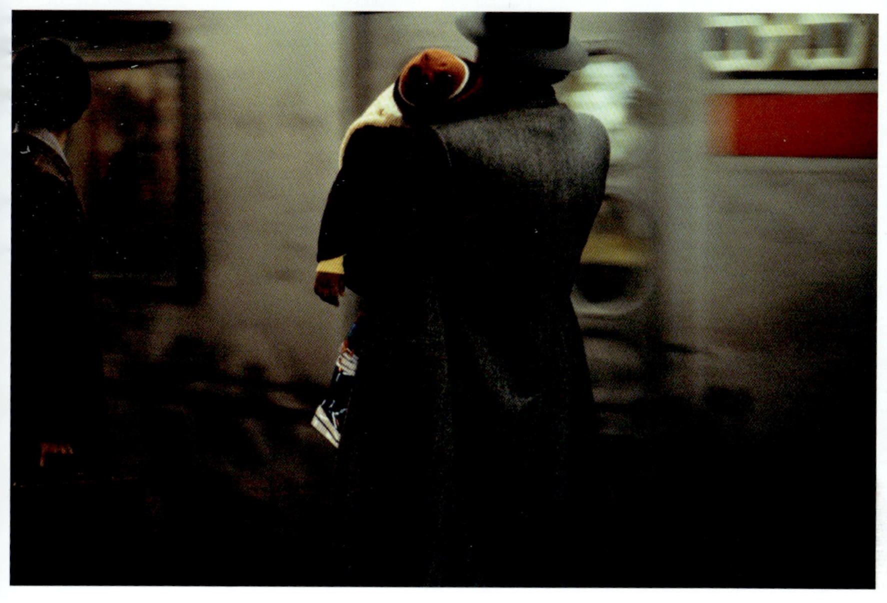

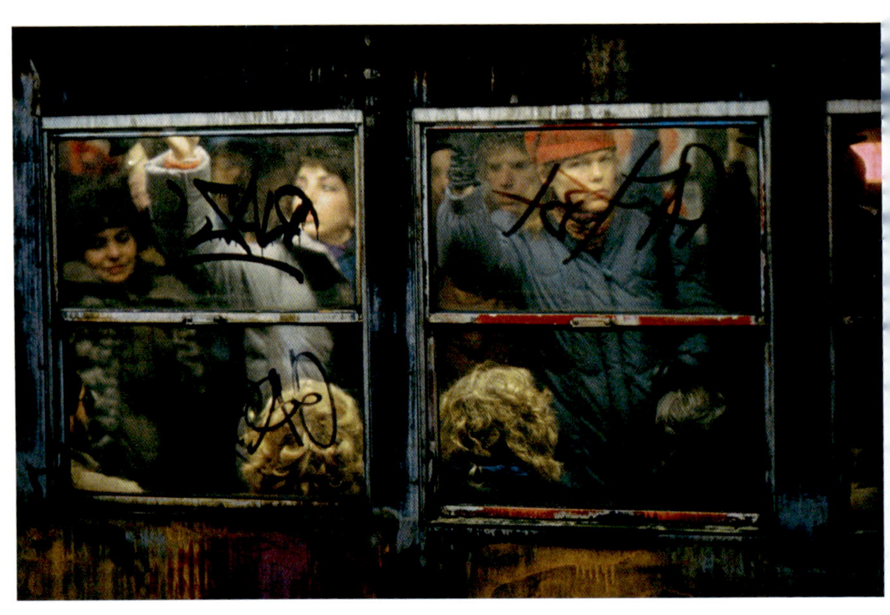

73. New York, 1982.
74. New York, 1985.

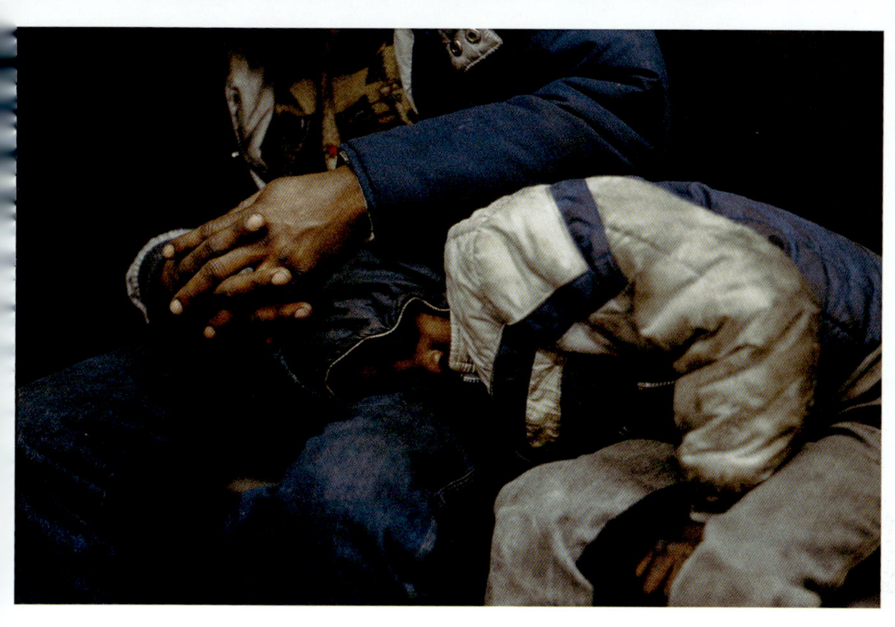

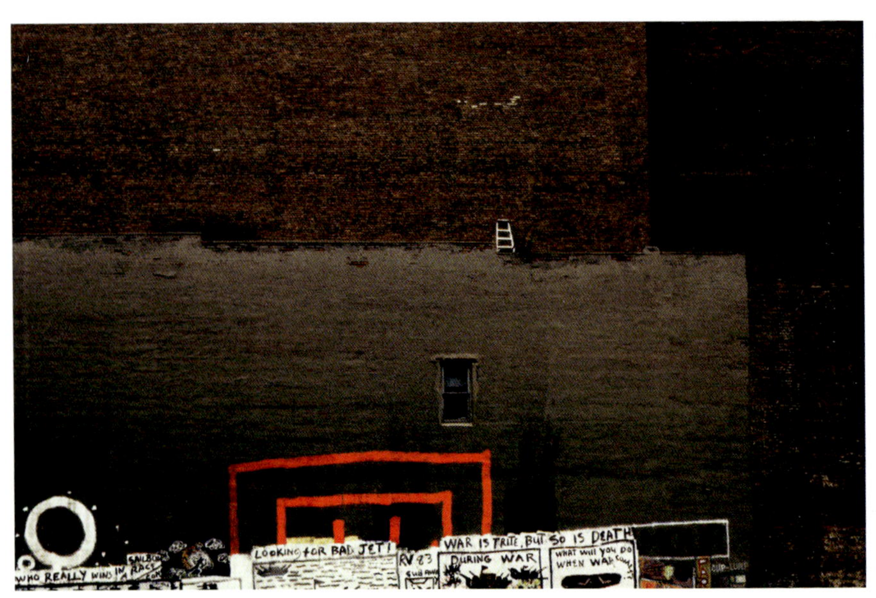

75. New York, 1984.
76. New York, 1986.

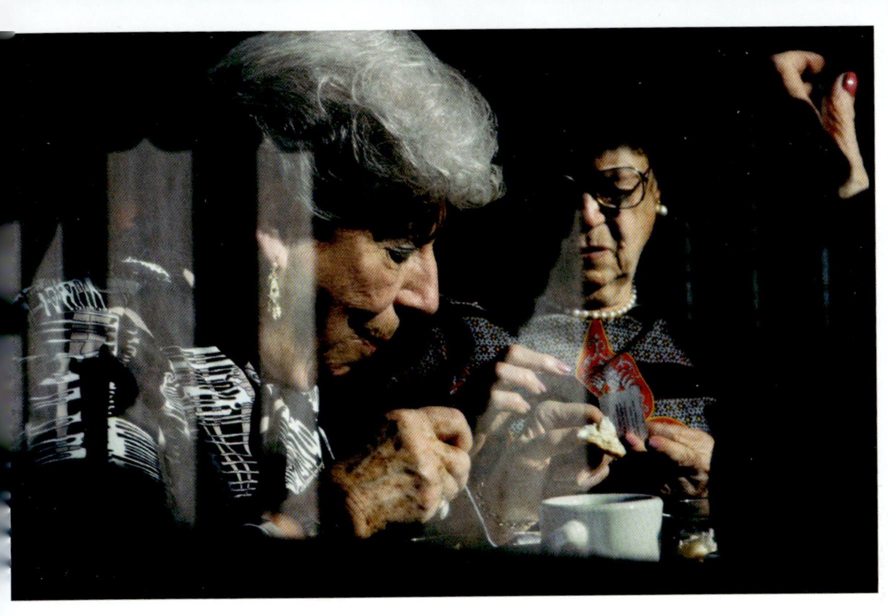

77. New York, 1984.

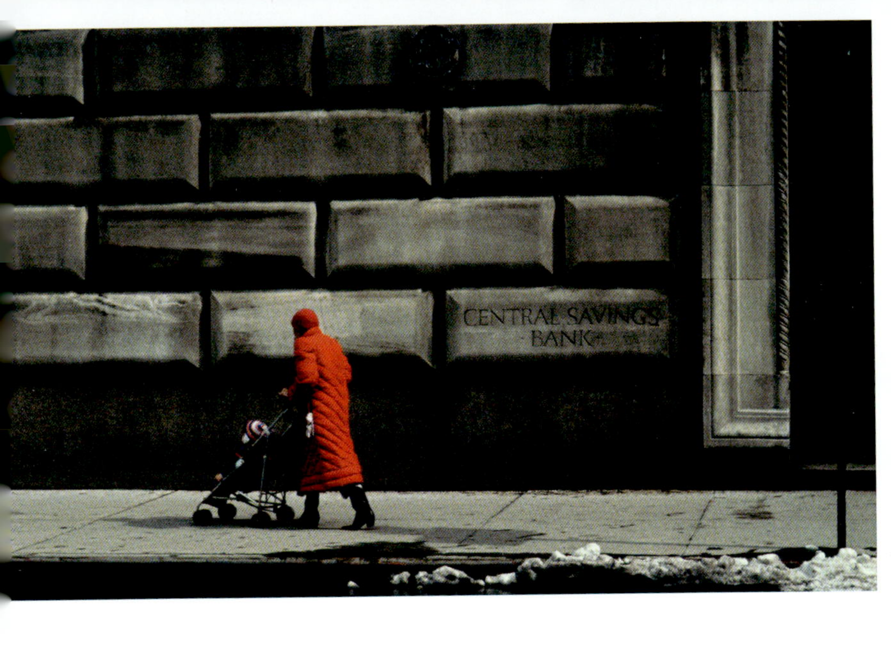

CENTRAL SAVINGS
BANK

Biography

1928 Francesco Horvat is born in Abbazia, Italy (present-day Opatija, Croatia) on 28 April, to Jewish parents of Central European origin.

1938 Racial laws targeting Jews are imposed in Italy.

1939 Horvat's father flees to Hungary where he survives the war thanks to false papers. His mother escapes to Switzerland with their two children.

1939–45 Attends middle school and then the local high school in Lugano. Swaps his stamp collection for a 35 mm Retinamat camera.

1945 Goes to Zurich.

1947 Enrols at the Brera Academy of Fine Arts in Milan but soon gives up his studies.

1948 Joins a small advertising agency where he is entrusted with commercial work and then some photographs. Acquires a Rolleicord 6 x 6.

1949 Visits his father, who has emigrated to Israel. First reportage work.

1951 First publication of his work, in black and white and in colour, in the Milanese magazine *Epoca*, under the name of Franco Horvat. In Paris, he meets Henri Cartier-Bresson, who advises him to buy a Leica and to go the Louvre to look at paintings by Poussin. Reportage on the Charlie de Beistegui Ball in Venice for the magazine *Point de Vue-Images du Monde* and first commission for the Swiss magazine *Die Woche*.

1952–54 Travels to Pakistan and then India, sending photographs to *Die Woche* and several press agencies in Paris, Munich, London and New York. His work features numerous times in *Sie und Er*, *Die Woche*, *Paris-Match*, *Picture Post*, *Münchner Illustrierte*, *L'Illustré*, *Life*, *Jubilee*, *L'illustrazione italiana*, *Frankfurter Illustrierte*, *Le Ore*, *The Sphere*.

1954 After travelling through Israel and Jordan, leaves for London, under contract with the American agency Black Star. Adopts the name Frank Horvat.

1955 An image he took in Pakistan is included in the exhibition *The Family of Man* at MoMA, New York. Photo essays published in *Collier's*, *VI*, *Hören und Sehen*, *Der Spiegel*, *Revue*, *Illustrated*, *Zondagsvriend*, *Esquire*, *Life*. Settles in Paris.

1956 Marries Maria Teresa (Mate) Lorenzetti. They have three children: Michel (1956), Lorenzo (1957) and Marco (1961). Reportages on prostitution and striptease. First commissions for the magazine *Réalités*. Shoots many images of Paris using a telephoto lens.

1957 His Paris pictures are published in the international magazine *Camera* and exhibited at the first Photography Biennale in Venice. Beginning of a collaboration with Jacques Moutin, art director of *Jardin des Modes*, who grants him recognition for his fashion photographs shot with the Leica.

1958 Begins a collaboration with *Jours de France* and *Elle*.

1959 His work is published in *Elle*, *Jardin des modes*, *Magnum* and *Jours de France*. Shoots photo stories on Paris, the suburbs, London and the Borinage region of Belgium for *Réalités*.

1960 First collaboration with *Vogue* UK, which brings him international fame in fashion circles. Becomes a Magnum associate.

1961–62 Leaves Magnum. Collaborations with *Glamour* and *Harper's Bazaar*.

1962–63 Photo essay on twelve great cities of the world for the German magazine *Revue*.

1967 Separates from Mate Lorenzetti. Birth of a son, David, with the model Marie-Louise Pierson.

1970 Acquires an isolated house in the Haut-Var region which he names La Véronique, like his partner Véronique Aubry.

1976 Travels around the world shooting portraits of trees, his first project in colour in collaboration with Michel Fresson.

1979 Birth of a daughter, Sarah Fiammetta, with Alexandra de Leal.

1982 Begins the series *Very Similar* and *New York Up & Down*. Buys a computer.

1983 Start of a collaboration with the *Frankfurter Allgemeine Zeitung* weekly supplement.

1986–87 *Entre Vues* project: interviews other photographers and starts his own personal collection of photographs.

1987 Finishes building a studio in Boulogne-Billancourt.

1989–90 Works with digital images and Photoshop, on projects including *Bestiary*.

1992 Joins the editorial board of the magazine *Photographers International*, Taiwan, founded by Nathalie Juan and Juan I-Jong.

1999 Creates a daily photo diary to commemorate the end of the millennium.

2003 Marries Véronique Aubry at Cotignac town hall. Begins the 'La Véronique' project, following a period of convalescence in the Var region.

2007 Begins the 'Eye at the Fingertips' project, which he pursues until the end of his life.

2012 Creates his own iPad app, 'Horvatland'.

2009–20 Self-publishes his collection of 'white books' (Only For Few collection).

2020 Dies on 21 October.

Selected Bibliography

Monographs

La Capture des éléphants sauvages,
   Paris: Louvois, 1957
Arbres, Nantes: Musée des Arts Décoratifs,
   1977
The Tree, text by John Fowles, London:
   Aurum Press; New York: Little Brown, 1979
*Goethe in Sicilia. Venti fotografie di Frank
   Horvat*, Palermo: Novecento, 1982
Frank Horvat, côté mode et *L'Album de famille*,
   text by Patrick Roegiers, Paris: Espace
   Photographique de la Ville de Paris/Paris
   Audiovisuel, 1989
Entre Vues, Paris: Nathan, 1990; new ed. 1991;
   Taipei: Photographer Publications, 1991
Frank Horvat, text by Jean Dieuzaide, Toulouse:
   Galerie Municipale du Château d'Eau, 1991
Arbres, text by Michel Cazenave, Paris:
   Imprimerie Nationale, 1994
Le Bestiaire d'Horvat, text by Pierre Gascar,
   Arles: Actes Sud, 1994
Paris Londres/London Paris, 1952–1962, Paris:
   Musée Carnavalet/Paris-Musées, 1996
Fifty-one photographs in black & white,
   Manchester: Dewi Lewis; Rome: Peliti
   Associati, 1998
Very Similar/Vraies Semblances, Paris: Galerie
   Dina Vierny; New ed. Rome: Peliti Associati;
   Seville: Photovision; Manchester: Dewi
   Lewis, 1999
1999, un journal photographique, Paris:
   Fondation Dina Vierny/Musée Maillol;
   Arles: Actes Sud, 2000; *1999, a daily report*,
   Manchester: Dewi Lewis, 2000; *1999,
   Ein Tagebuch*, Heidelberg: Braus, 2000
Alain d'Hoogue, *Frank Horvat*, 'Photo Poche'
   series, Paris: Nathan, 2000
Strip-tease, Paris: Galerie Dina Vierny, 2001
Figures romanes, text by Michel Pastoureau,
   Paris: Seuil, 2001
Time Machine, Only For Few collection
   (self-published), 2004
Horvat photographie Couturier, Paris:
   Gallimard/Musée Maillol, 2005

Le labyrinthe Horvat, text by Martin Harrison,
   Paris: Éditions du Chêne/Hachette, 2006
À hauteur d'arbres, Paris: La Martinière,
   2008
Frank Horvat, un regard sur les années 60,
   foreword by Giovanna Calvenzi, Barcelona:
   Loft Publications; Paris: Cyel Éditions, 2012
La Maison aux quinze clefs, foreword by
   Jean-Noël Jeanneney, Paris: Éditions
   Terre Bleue, 2013
Please don't smile, text by Matthias Harder,
   Ostfildern: Hatje Cantz, 2015
Photographic Autobiography, Ostfildern:
   Hatje Cantz, 2016
Frank Horvat, Turin: Musei Reali/Silvana
   Editoriale, 2018
New York Up & Down, text by Roger Szmulewicz
   and Vince Aletti, Antwerp: Gallery Fifty One,
   2018
Un moment d'une femme, Tokyo: Chanel
   Nexus Hall, 2018
Side Walk, Paris: Éditions Xavier-Barral;
   Ostfildern: Hatje Cantz, 2020
Frank Horvat 50–65, text by Quentin Bajac,
   Virginie Chardin and Susanna Brown,
   Paris: Jeu de Paume/La Martinière, 2022

Other publications

The Family of Man, text by Edward Steichen,
   New York: Museum of Modern Art, 1955
J'aime la télévision, text by Max Egly, Lausanne:
   Éditions Rencontre; Paris: Denoël, 1962
J'aime le 'striptease', text by Patrick
   Lindermohr, Lausanne: Éditions
   Rencontre; Paris: Denoël, 1962
Martin Harrison, *Shots of Style, Great Fashion
   Photographs Chosen by David Bailey*,
   London: Victoria & Albert Museum, 1985
'Tête-à-tête avec Frank Horvat', in *Photo
   Magazine*, nos. 65, 66, 68, 1985
Martin Harrison, *Appearances, Fashion
   Photography since 1945*, London: Jonathan
   Cape, 1991
'Frank Horvat, Photobiographie', interview with

Loïc Metayer, *France Photographie*,
   no. 133, 1993
Anne de Mondenard and Michel Guerrin,
   *'Réalités': un mensuel français illustré,
   1946–1978*, Paris: Maison Européenne de
   la Photographie; Arles: Actes Sud, 2008
Sophie Bernard, 'Les vies de Frank Horvat',
   in *Camera*, no. 13, 2008
Hans-Michael Koetzle, *Eyes Wide Open!
   100 years of Leica Photography*, Berlin:
   Kehrer, 2017
*Icons of Style: A Century of Fashion
   Photography*, text by Paul Martineau,
Susanna Brown *et al.*, Los Angeles:
J. Paul Getty Museum, 2018

TV and radio

2000 *1999, Un journal photographique*,
   directed by Annabelle Le Doeuff, Arte
2014 *Frank Horvat*, documentary in the series
   À voix nue, interview with Amaury Chardeau,
   5 episodes, each 28 mins, France Culture
2015 *Portrait de photographe: Frank Horvat*,
   directed by Philippe Abergel, 26 mins
2018 *Le Photosophe, des instants avec Frank
   Horvat*, film by Sandra Wis, Wis Films, 72 mins

Selected Exhibitions

Solo exhibitions

1977 *Arbres*, Musée des Arts Décoratifs, Nantes; International Center of Photography, New York, 1978; Photographers' Gallery, London, 1978; Artcurial, Paris, 1980; Galleria Novecento, Palermo, 1981; Zeit Gallery, Tokyo, 1981

1980 *30 Happy Years*, Photographers Gallery, London; *30 années de bonheur*, Galerie Mamiya, Paris, 1981

1983 *Vraies Semblances*, Espace Canon, Paris; *Very Similar*, Photokina, Cologne and Galleria Novecento, Palermo, 1986; Fotofest, Houston, 1990; Fotografie Forum, Frankfurt, 1997; Hackelbury Fine Arts, London, 1999; Galerie Dina Vierny, Paris, 2002

1989 *Frank Horvat côté mode*, Espace Photographique de la Ville de Paris

1991 *Frank Horvat*, Galerie Municipale du Château d'Eau, Toulouse

1994 *Le Bestiaire d'Horvat/Horvat's Bestiary*, Centre National de la Photographie, Paris; Centro Krizia, Milan, 1995; Multimedia Art Museum, Moscow, 2021

1995 *Please Don't Smile, Fashion Photos*, Hamiltons Gallery, London; Staley-Wise Gallery, New York; Carla Sozzani, Milan; Agathe Gaillard, Paris

1996 *Paris Londres/London Paris, 1952–1962*, Musée Carnavalet, Paris

1997 *Black and White Photographs 1952/1964*, Fotografie Forum, Frankfurt; Hackelbury, London, 2002

1997 *Vintage Prints*, Staley-Wise Gallery, New York

1998 *51 photographies en noir et blanc*, Galerie Esther Woerdehoff, Paris; Galeria Railowski, Valencia; In Focus Gallery, Cologne, 2000; Hackelbury Gallery, London, 2002; Fifty-One Gallery, Antwerp, 2002

1999 *Goethe en Sicile*, Maison de Goethe, Rome

2000 *1999, un journal photographique*, Fondation Dina Vierny/Musée Maillol, Paris

2000 *New York Up & Down*, Stadtgalerie, Kiel

2001 *Strip Tease*, Galerie Dina Vierny, Paris; Staley-Wise Gallery, New York, 2002

2003 *Les 75 printemps de Frank Horvat*, Maison de la Photographie, Toulon

2004 *La Véronique*, Galerie Dina Vierny, Paris

2006 *Le labyrinthe Horvat*, Espace Landowski, Boulogne-Billancourt

2008 *Horvat, les voies d'un regard*, Villa Tamaris, La Seyne-sur-Mer

2009 *De-bocche-tette-culi-cazzi-e-mone*, Galerie Dina Vierny, Paris

2010 *Fashion Photography*, Manège Gallery, St Petersburg

2011 *No Repeat 1945–2010*, Craf, Spilimbergo

2012 *Fashion Photographs*, Presentation House Gallery, Vancouver

The iPad Exhibition: A Trip Through a Mind, Galerie Hiltawsky, Berlin

Trip to Carrara, Galerie Dina Vierny, Paris

2013 *La Maison aux quinze clefs*, Galerie Dina Vierny, Paris; Théâtre de la Photographie et de l'Image, Nice, 2014

Look Ma! No Hands, Galerie Dina Vierny, Paris

2014 *House with Fifteen Keys*, Palazzo Mediceo, Seravezza; Helmut Newton Foundation, Berlin, 2015; Multimedia Art Museum, Moscow, 2019

2018 *Un moment d'une femme*, Chanel Nexus Hall, Tokyo; Kyotographie, Kyoto

Frank Horvat, storia di un fotografo, Musei Reali, Turin

Frank Horvat et ses contemporains, Vieille Église St Vincent, Mérignac; Maison de la Photographie, Lille

2020 *Paris années 50*, Maison de la Photographie Robert Doisneau, Gentilly

2022 *Frank Horvat 50–65*, Jeu de Paume, Château de Tours

Group exhibitions

1955 *The Family of Man,* Museum of Modern Art, New York

1957 1st Biennial Exhibition of Photography, Venice

1958 *12 International Photographers*, Värmlands Museum, Karlstad

1961 *Métamorphose et invention d'un visage*, 14th International Salon of Portrait Photography, Bibliothèque Nationale, Paris

1964 *What Is Man?*, international touring photography exhibition, curated by Karl Pawek, in the style of *The Family of Man*

1977 *La Deuxième Génération de la photographie en couleur*, Rencontres Internationales de la Photographie, Arles

1981 *Paris, Paris: créations en France, 1937–1957*, Centre Georges Pompidou, Paris

1985 *Shots of Style: Great Fashion Photographs Chosen by David Bailey*, Victoria & Albert Museum, London

1991 *Appearances: Fashion Photography since 1945*, Victoria and Albert Museum, London

1994 *Vanités, photographies de mode des XIXe et XXe siècles*, Centre National de la Photographie, Paris

2006 *Indianscope*, Maison de la Photographie du Nord-Pas-de-Calais, Lille

2018 *Icons of Style. A Century of Fashion Photography*, J. Paul Getty Museum, Los Angeles